Savvy Girl

a. Guide to

WINE

BRITTANY DEAL

Content Editor: Meghan Rabbitt
Copyeditor: Rachelle Mandik
Cover and Interior Design: Tara Long/Dotted Line Design, llc

Savvy Girl.
1600 Main St., Los Angeles, CA 90291
www.savvygirl.net

Ordering Information:
Orders by U.S. trade bookstores and wholesalers.
Please visit CreateSpace.com.

Published in the United States of America
ISBN 978-0-9897109-0-9
First Edition

#hashtags

#yumoryuck #yum #yuck #brittanydeal #goodread
#savvygirl #winebook #sassinaglass #wine
#winetastingparty #getsavvy #wino #iheartwine
#winewednesdays #winetastingtuesdays #winetastingthursdays
#winenot? #savvygirlguides
#mybuzzwordisbetterthanyours #makethosetanninspurr
#winegetaways #savvygirlwine #winecountry
#winelover #shortbook #catpeeonagooseberrybush

[#getsavvy]

WHAT IS SAVVY GIRL?

Brittany, a lifetime lover of learning, craved the knowledge how-to books promised to offer, but found them painful to complete. Sometimes her sheer pride would hold her hostage until she finished all 329 pages, but once she was freed, she wondered if "boring" was a requirement for getting a book published.

Sure, searching Google is another way to get quickie how-tos, but who wants to sift through a million search results or keyword-stuffed blogs?

After giving up on another how-to book in the Bolivian Amazon, Brittany realized that people are drowning in information, yet starved for knowledge.

With the idea of creating one "go-to" source for rich, yet concise, knowledge on the topics women care about, Brittany launched Savvy Girl. The Savvy Girl promise is to produce a book that you can start on a Monday and finish by Friday. Why so short? Because most of us don't want to be an expert on every topic, we just want to be savvy.

So read 'em, get savvy, and then get back to your fabulous life.

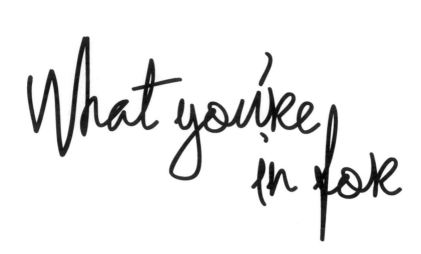

What you're in for

Wine 101

IS IT YUM OR YUCK?

It was a sunny spring afternoon in Napa, California, when I arrived at a small boutique winery nestled among the region's famous rolling green vineyards. As I walked up the cobblestone entrance lined by rows of lavender, the smell of red wine and oak barrels led me to the tasting room.

I introduced myself to the woman behind the bar and casually mentioned I was writing a book on wine. "Fantastic," she said. "Our winemaker is in the tasting room today, so I will have her join us."

Instead of excitement, this news brought anxiety. My afternoon of wine tasting on a workday had just turned into a pop quiz, and I started to wonder whether I'd absorbed anything from all of the wine books I'd been reading.

The winemaker poured me a taste of her Sauvignon Blanc and read me the tasting notes: "A dry wine with aromas of citrus fruits, and a hint of grass." Wanting to look like a pro, I vigorously swirled the wine in my glass and then carefully smelled the wine.

After taking in the wine's aromas (and wondering where that hint of grass was hiding), I took a small sip and swished the wine to all the areas of my tongue. As I desperately searched for something clever to say, the winemaker smiled and said, "Well . . . is it yum or yuck?"

All of my anxiety melted away as I gratefully answered, "Yum!" Her question made me realize how fancy wine jargon can make us forget the most important question to answer when it comes to wine: Do we like it or not?

While keeping this most important question in mind, the following pages will fill you in on all the wine basics you want to know, such as how to describe the wines you like, how to read a wine label, and of course, how to sound like the Savvy Girl you are when ordering wine at a restaurant.

After you've finished this book, if you ever feel like wine is getting a bit too complicated, just pour yourself another glass and remember that even winemakers know the bottom line on wine is simply this: Is it yum or yuck?

HOW WINE ALMOST BECAME EXTINCT

It's hard to imagine a world without wine; I mean, what else would we use to help us decipher the meaning of life, cope with dating mishaps, or get through an episode of *The Bachelor*? But here's the thing: Not too long ago, wine nearly became extinct.

It was the end of the nineteenth century in France and, out of nowhere, vineyard after vineyard began to eerily die off. The cause of the vineyard devastation was eventually linked to a tiny parasite called phylloxera, which feasted on the roots of the vines, literally sucking the life out of them.

Soon, phylloxera spread across Europe, wiping out more than 70 percent of the wine industry. Understandably, wine lovers became desperate for a solution. The French government even offered a large monetary prize to whoever could solve the mystery, but nothing seemed to work. Everyone thought wine was a goner. But at the eleventh hour, two researchers, entomologist Charles Valentine Riley and botanist Jules Émile Planchon, swooped in with a clever idea.

The solution involved taking vine cuttings from French grape vines and grafting them onto the rootstock of a native North American species whose roots were so thick, phylloxera couldn't gnaw through them. This worked because the Frankenstein's monster–like plant was able to survive in the presence of phylloxera, and the grafted vines were still able to produce the same quality of fruit—despite growing on foreign roots. Although no one ever figured out how to completely wipe out phylloxera, experts credit Riley and Planchon for saving the wine industry.

You might be wondering why winemakers didn't just use the North American grapevine species to make wine. "The reason is because

how to graft a vine

many of these North American species produce grapes that are worse than bad—they are *terrible*," says Dr. Andy Walker, a professor in the Viticulture and Enology Program at UC-Davis (the number-one wine program in the United States). "Not only do the wines from these grapes taste foul, but fruit from some of them also contains calcium oxalate, which makes your tongue and throat swell." Yikes.

Considering Dr. Walker's explanation, it's clear that the right grapevines are needed to make wine worth drinking. But having the right vines isn't the only thing that contributes to good wine. Each step of the winemaking process—from growing the grapes to aging the wine—affects how the wine will taste.

HOW GOOD WINE IS MADE: FROM VINE TO WINE

Here's how the four-step process from vine to wine affects taste:

STEP 1 ▸ GROW DELICIOUS, RIPE GRAPES

Gerard Zanzonico, a thirty-year winemaking veteran and current winemaker at Del Dotto Vineyards in Napa Valley, California, says,

"The number-one determiner of quality in a wine is the quality of the grapes you start with." That's why a winemaker must know how his vineyards are doing at all times, he says, because ultimately, wine is made in the vineyard.

"Take a peach pie for example," says Zanzonico. "You can't make a delicious peach pie with bad peaches, and it's the same concept with wine. You can't make good wine from bad grapes."

So, how does one grow good grapes?

GOOD GRAPES THRIVE IN FABULOUS TERROIR

Although wine is made around the world, wine grapes can't be grown just anywhere. Grapevines don't exactly get along with the *terroir* of the snowcapped mountains of Alaska or the arid deserts of the Sahara.

This difficult-to-pronounce word "terroir" (you can thank the French for that one) means everything environmentally about a location that affects how a grape grows, such as sunshine, rainfall, cloud cover, wind, soil, and even the altitude of the vineyard or angle to the sun. Together, all of these elements influence the flavor of a wine, which is why winemakers care so much about where the grapes are planted. Essentially, the better the terroir, the better the grape; the better the grape, the better the wine.

Since every terroir is unique, the same varietal (type of grape) can taste quite different from one place to another (for example, think of a Sauvignon Blanc from Napa Valley compared to a Sauvignon Blanc from New Zealand). The best way to understand how terroir can make the same varietal taste different is to compare terroir to how culture affects the development of a person. For example, think about how people like to settle in the suburbs, or in certain cities, because of how the area's culture—its terroir, you could say—will affect the development of their children.

The same way that not all families thrive in the same suburbs or cities, not all grape varietals do well in the same terroir. For each varietal to thrive, the terroir must be the right match for its growing preferences.

Have you ever heard that Oregon is known for Pinot Noir, and California is known for Zinfandel? When a winemaker plays Cupid and pairs the grape varietal with its terroir match, their little grapes grow up and thrive, and wine regions become known for certain wines.

GOOD GRAPES NEED THEIR VITAMIN D

Grapes need sunlight in order to ripen and develop enough sugar. To help grapes get their tan on, winemakers will spread the vines along a trellis, and remove excess leaves (this is referred to as "canopy management").

Although all grapes need sunlight to ripen, not all are beach bunnies. Pinot Noir likes cooler temperatures because its thin skin is sensitive to the sun. That grape reminds me of my Polish cousins, who have such pale skin they manage to sunburn on cloudy days.

GOOD GRAPES THRIVE WHEN FACED WITH A LITTLE ADVERSITY

Turns out Friedrich Nietzsche's famous quote "That which does not kill us makes us stronger" also applies to grapevines. Contrary to what you would expect, grapevines don't produce the best grapes in luscious, fertile land where nutrients are handed to them on a silver platter.

The grapes that turn out best are the ones that experience a little vineyard "stress" that makes them work for their nutrients. A good example of vineyard stress is soil with good drainage. When less water is readily available for the grapevines, they have to send their roots deeper into the soil in search of nutrients and water. This creates a strong root base, and the stronger the root base, the better the vines will be at creating juicy grapes that'll turn into wine you'll love.

STEP 2 ▸ PICK THE GRAPES

A grape's peak ripeness is a matter of personal taste rather than an exact science, so choosing when to harvest the grapes is a skill that each winemaker has to develop.

As a grape ripens, it becomes sweeter, but at the cost of losing its sourness (called *acidity* in wine-speak). Choosing the right balance between sweetness and acidity is part of what makes good wine good. It's kind of like lemonade: Too much sugar and it'll taste too sweet; too much lemon juice and it'll taste too tart. The perfect balance of sugar and acidity not only makes great lemonade, but also great wine.

Wino Buzzword

BRIX: In the United States, Brix is a measure of the sugar level in wine grapes before they are harvested. Winemakers use Brix measurements to help them decide when to harvest.

STEP 3 ▸ SQUASH AND FERMENT THE GRAPES

Finally, we're on to the fun part: where grape juice turns into wine.

Once the grapes are harvested, they're placed into large containers and compressed so that the juice is released. You know that iconic scene from *I Love Lucy* where she stomps on the grapes? Yeah, if you end up doing that on a wine-tasting trip, know that you're doing it just for the kitsch factor. The good old foot-stomping days are pretty much over thanks to today's technology, which helps winemakers compress tons of grapes much more efficiently than a barefoot romp in a vat of grapes.

Once the grapes are crushed, the fermentation (aka alcohol-makin') process begins. Grape juice becomes wine with the help of living organisms called yeasts, which exist naturally on the skins of the grapes. During fermentation, the yeasts eat the sugar in the grape juice and turn it into alcohol. Once this process is complete—anywhere from a few days to a few months—the yeasts die and fall to the bottom of the grape-juice-turned-alcohol mixture.

In addition to the yeast that's naturally present on the skins of the grapes (aka native yeast), winemakers will sometimes add processed native yeast to the grape juice. Dr. Linda Bisson, a professor at UC Davis who specializes in yeast microbiology, told me that the processed native yeast originally came from a vineyard but were later processed and bred by researchers for ideal qualities (kind of like dogs), such as aromas and fermentation efficiency. The reason some winemakers choose to use the processed native yeast over the natural yeast in their vineyard is to have more control over the taste of their wine.

Once the juice becomes wine, it's moved to either steel containers or oak barrels for aging.

STEP 4 ▸ AGE THE WINE

In the same way that teenagers head off to college to grow up before they enter the real world, wine needs time to get its act together before bottling. The maturation period for wine can vary, similar to the way some people (say, frat boys) need a little more time to mature than others.

Before bottling, wines mature in either steel containers or in oak barrels. Stainless-steel containers help to preserve the natural fruity aromas in a wine, while oak barrels add toasty, buttery, and, well, oaky flavors to a wine.

FRENCH VERSUS AMERICAN OAK

Oak barrels used to age wine are most commonly made from either American oak or French oak. I know what you're thinking: Oak is oak, right? Well, not exactly. In the same way that terroir gives grapes their distinctive flavors, terroir does the same thing for oak trees.

Flash back to fourth grade with me for a second here: Remember learning about how you can tell a tree's age by counting the rings around the center of the stump? Well, these growth rings affect the oak's grain, which will translate to different flavors and textures in wine that's been aged in oak.

For example, in a warm climate, an oak tree's growth rings are farther apart; in a cold climate, they're closer together. French oak trees grow in a cool climate, so they have a tighter grain, which lends subtle, silky, and spicy notes to a wine. American oak trees, on the other hand, grow in warmer climates, so they have a looser grain, which lends more bold flavors of vanilla and coconut as well as creamier textures to a wine.

TANNIN: THE CHEESE TO A RED WINE'S MACARONI

You are the cheese to my macaroni. You are the horizon to my sky. You are the bacon to my eggs. You are the laces to my sneakers. You are the jelly to my peanut butter. You are the smile to my face. You are the gravy to my mashed potatoes You are the bubbles to my bath. You are the milk to my cookie. You are the ink to my pen. You are the ketchup to my french fries. You are the water to my ocean. You are the icing on my cupcake.

I love mac and cheese, but without the cheese, those semicircle noodles don't quite have the same appeal. Tannins, like cheese, add a lot of flavor to a red wine, and they are the reason why many people prefer reds to whites.

Tannins are pigmented compounds in the skins of the grapes—essentially what make red wines red. But tannins add so much more to red wine than color; they also add texture, body, and complexity.

RED, RED WINE

The juice of both green and purple wine grapes is typically colorless. Red wines get their color from being in contact with their purple skins during the fermentation process. The longer the wine is kept in contact with its skins, the more tannins—and therefore color—will be absorbed. For example, rosé wines are made from red wine grapes, and only spend a brief time in contact with their skins. Meanwhile, white wine is fermented from white grapes and *without* their skins, which is why there is little tannin in white wines.

TANNIN'S GOT FANGS

Have you ever taken a sip of red wine and suddenly become keenly aware of your tongue, cheeks, and the roof of your mouth? This drying-out sensation—which kind of feels like you just sucked on a cotton ball—is what gives red wine "structure." It's a careful balance, though, because while the right level of structure from tannins imparts boldness and richness to a red wine, too much can feel like the wine is attacking your mouth.

To make those harsh tannins purr (meaning relax and soften), people often decant a tannic red wine before drinking it. (More on decanting later.)

CURVALICIOUS

Tannins affect the "body" of a wine, also known as the weight of the wine in your mouth. Grapes with thicker and darker skins, such as a Cabernet Sauvignon, will have higher levels of tannins, and thus feel heavier (these are often called "full-bodied" reds). Grapes with thinner and lighter-colored skins, like Pinot Noir, have fewer tannins and feel lighter (and are often referred to as "light-bodied" wines).

BETTER IN TIME

The tannins in red wine act like a natural preservative, helping red wines improve with age. Over time, those feisty tannins become softer and more integrated in the wine, creating deliciously complex flavors.

Next Up

→ Why do wine snobs swirl their wine? Is it just for show?

→ Did you know that most of what we taste is actually what we smell?

→ Learn how Jennifer Simonetti-Bryan, the fourth woman in the United States to earn the Master of Wine title, was able to identify thirty-six wines blind—and how you can learn to train your own palate.

Parlez-Vous Wine Speak?

After spending countless hours reading about wine and just as much time drinking wine—I mean *practicing*—it wasn't hard to toss out some buzzwords, but accurately applying them was another story.

So I did what any Savvy Girl who'd just quit her banking job to write a book on wine would do: I signed up for an adult education course on wine. What I called important research, my parents called taking their "follow your passion" advice too literally.

In class I learned a lot of information about wine regions and types of wine, but the best lesson came from the girl who sat next to me.

It was a Thursday evening, and our class was held in the basement of an old, neglected college building. The three-hour class began with two painstaking hours of PowerPoint slides before our teacher finally let us drink—I mean *taste*.

The wine that stood out was an inky-purple, full-bodied Syrah. As we sniffed the wine, our teacher asked us what aromas we could

16

identify. That's when the girl sitting next to me blurted out, "Slim Jim."

Amused, our teacher said, "So, perhaps a meaty or gamey aroma?"

The girl shrugged and said, "Eh, I still get Slim Jim."

Once she let Slim Jim out of the bag, that was all I could smell in that wine—a pungent, savory, peppery piece of beef.

Was "Slim Jim" an appropriate descriptor for this wine? Absolutely. Not only will we sometimes detect different aromas from our friends while tasting the same wine, but we will also use different words to describe the same thing. I knew someone who once likened the aromas of Chardonnay she tried to pancakes. To her, something about the caramel, oaky aromas reminded her of the maple syrup on her pancakes.

So, whether you find yourself describing a wine with eloquent adjectives like "gamey" or "oaky"—or you sniff more "Slim Jim" or "pancakes"—just remember that whatever adjective *you* come up with to describe a wine is just fine.

The best way to get better at describing what you taste is to try lots of wine and practice using words—any words—to describe your experience. The more you do it, the better you'll get at it. For example, once you can identify a certain aroma in a wine, it's easier to find it the next time.

Before you go wine tasting or hit your local grocery store for a variety of their $10-and-under bottles, there are some helpful tricks to get you started on learning how to taste and talk about wine like someone who knows her stuff.

You might as well open a bottle as you read this chapter. After all, practice makes perfect.

HOW TO TASTE WINE: THE FIVE S'S

You've probably watched this happen at some point: A sophisticated-looking guy orders a glass of expensive wine, eagerly swirls the wine in his glass, then puts his nose so deep in the glass you'd think he was going to use it as a straw. He takes several long sniffs and after a brief moment of intense contemplation, you see him take a delicate sip followed by a swishing noise as he loudly moves the wine around in his mouth. Finally, he swallows the wine as his lips twist into a smirk that seems to imply he might have just found where that "hint of grass" was hiding. And maybe you've even pegged that guy as a total wine snob. (I know I have.)

The reason wine snobs and sommeliers do this whole swirl 'n' sip charade is because it helps them slow down and pay attention to the wine, so they can find the words to describe it. Sommeliers get good at identifying aromas in a wine not because they have a better sense of smell than the rest of us, but because they taste with *focused attention.*

So while you don't have to make your wine tasting as dramatic as "that guy," you might want to slow your tasting down a touch. That's because no two wines are the same, and learning how to describe what you taste will help you develop your palate—and ultimately help you find what style of wine you like best.

DEVELOPING YOUR PALATE:

See ▸ Swirl ▸ Sniff ▸ Sip ▸ Scrutinize

SEE ▸ HERE'S WHERE YOU DESCRIBE A WINE'S APPEARANCE

Confession time: I find describing a wine's appearance a waste of time. Why? Well, the color doesn't affect the smell or taste of a wine.

That being said, in case you find yourself in a blind tasting—or you just want to impress your friends—here are a few "trivia" points you may want to know about a wine's appearance:

WHAT THE COLOR CAN TELL YOU ABOUT THE VARIETAL: Different grape varieties give different colors. For example, Chardonnay has a deeper color than Sauvignon Blanc, especially when the wine is aged in oak barrels.

champagne   sauvignon blanc   pinot grigio   chardonnay

rosé   pinot noir   merlot   cabernet sauvignon

As far as red wines go, if a red wine's color is more opaque, it will be a varietal with higher tannin levels, such as a Cabernet Sauvignon or a Syrah. If the color is more transparent, it's more likely a lighter-bodied red wine, such as a Pinot Noir.

WHAT THE COLOR CAN TELL YOU ABOUT THE AGE: White wine darkens with age and red wine lightens with age. In red wines, the grape-skin particles link up over time and fall to the bottom of the wine (the particles contain pigment and yank the color from the wine when they fall to the bottom). White wines darken with age due to oxidation (from the tiny bit of air between the wine and the cork), the same way an apple turns brown from oxidation after you cut it in half.

White wine darkens
as it ages

Red wine lightens
as it ages

If you only remember one tidbit about a wine's appearance, make it the part about how color tells you something about the age of the wine. If a wine connoisseur shares a bottle with you from her prized cellar, there's a good chance it'll be an aged red wine. A savvy remark about how red wine loses its color with age might get you invited back for more, since that kind of comment shows you "appreciate" good wine.

SWIRL ▸ HERE'S WHERE YOU START SWIRLING THAT WINEGLASS

To swirl, or not to swirl: That is the question. If it's a casual night with your girlfriends, don't worry about swirling, but if you splurged on a nice bottle or you're at a tasting, you definitely want to swirl.

savvy tip [Make sure to only fill the glass one-third full if you plan to swirl it, otherwise the wine will end up in your lap.]

I know that swirling can come off as pretentious, but there's a good reason for it. Swirling helps some of the wine evaporate, making the wine easier to smell. What you may not know is that our taste buds can only detect sweet, acidic, bitter, and salty flavors, so your cherry and lemon flavors are actually aromas you smell, not taste.

DID YOU KNOW...The reason we think we taste flavors is because we can detect smells via our *retronasal passageway*, the area between our nose and the back of our throat. When we sip wine, we breathe in its aromas, which travel up the retronasal passageway and into our nose, where we smell them, but since we smell those flavors while the wine is in our mouth, we think we taste them. This is why we plug our nose when swallowing icky medicine and why our food tastes bland when we get a cold.

There is one more thing you should know about swirling. The wine tears (or "legs," as some call it) that appear on the sides of your wineglass after swirling do not indicate a higher-quality wine, although some wine salespeople will try to use that one on you. The reason wine tears form on the glass has to do with how alcohol has a lower surface tension than water. Wine with higher alcohol levels produces more tears. The rest of the answer is pretty scientific and boring, so I'll spare you.

SNIFF ▸ HERE'S WHERE YOU SMELL THE WINE AND START TALKIN'

Have you ever smelled a wine and instantly identified a familiar aroma—but struggled to find the right word for it? Researchers hypothesize that aromas are hard to describe because smell, which is our most primitive sense, isn't well linked to the much newer verbal part of our brain. The weak link between these two areas of the brain makes it hard for us to use language to describe what we smell.

DID YOU KNOW...Some people refer to the aromas/smells of a wine as the wine's "nose."

Despite the inherent difficulty we all have when it comes to identifying aromas, everyone improves with practice. Take for example Jennifer Simonetti-Bryan, MW, one of the leading women in the wine industry. She's a Master of Wine, author of *The One Minute Wine Master* and *Pairing with the Masters: A Definitive Guide to Food & Wine*.

Before Simonetti-Bryan became a go-to wine guru, she started out as an investment banker. One day while attending a business lunch in London, she was served an herb-crusted salmon paired with a glass of Sancerre. The way the acid in the wine cut through the oil in the salmon and enhanced the flavors of both rocked her world; she knew she had to learn more about this wine thing.

Soon after that fateful lunch, she left her career in banking to pursue her new passion for wine. After many years of intense focus and studying, she became the fourth woman in the United States to earn the Master of Wine title—the highest title in the wine world, and one that fewer than three hundred people in the world hold. (Getting to put "MW" after your name involves passing a grueling four-day exam and identifying thirty-six wines *blind*. A mere 10 percent of people pass.)

I called Simonetti-Bryan to learn how she went from a sophisticated investment banker to a Jedi Wine Master (which is also her

Twitter handle), hoping she could shed some light on how I could improve my palate. Simonetti-Bryan told me that identifying aromas and learning to talk about wine is all about paying attention and training your palate. "In fact, I have an identical twin sister who can't identify wine aromas because she hasn't practiced," she said. "And we have the exact same DNA, so it's not that I have a better palate, I just have a *trained* palate."

When she was first starting out, Simonetti-Bryan purchased the Le Nez du Vin kit. This kit contains small jars with a range of different smells found in wine. She said she would practice with these kits and try to identify them blind. "Eventually, I would grab two at a time, such as cherry and hazelnut, and see if I could identify both smells together," she told me.

You don't need to buy the Le Nez du Vin kit to enjoy wine, but if you get bit by the wine bug or want a career in the wine industry, these kits can help you improve your sense of smell and your ability to describe wine aromas. For the rest of us who primarily want to drink wine, and maybe learn to describe what we like, my advice is to start out by saying whatever comes to your mind—just like that girl from my wine class who said she thought the Syrah smelled liked Slim Jim.

Worried that blurting out whatever comes to your mind might make you sound like an amateur? Just know that a British wine critic once likened a New Zealand Sauvignon Blanc to "cat pee on a gooseberry bush" (apparently a compliment).

A British wine critic once likened a New Zealand Sauvignon Blanc to "cat pee on a gooseberry bush"

If you find your imagination hasn't had its cup of coffee that day, try to think of a **F.E.W.** smells. Start with **F** for fruit aromas, **E** for earthy aromas, and **W** for winemaking-related aromas.

Fruit

BERRY FRUITS	**CITRUS FRUITS**	**STONE & TROPICAL FRUITS**
Raspberry	Grapefruit	(stone = fruits with a pit)
Cherry	Lemon	Peach
Strawberry	Lime	Apricot
Blackberry		Melon
Plum		Apple
Dried fruit		Pear
		Pineapple

Earth

EARTHY	**FLORAL**	**SPICY**
Herbs	Violet	Black pepper
Grass	Rose	Clove
Dried leaves	Orange blossom	Licorice
Mushrooms	Jasmine	

Winemaking

AROMAS FROM WINEMAKING TECHNIQUES

Vanilla	Oak	Tobacco
Melted butter	Cedar	Leather
Butterscotch	Chocolate	Petrol

SIP ▸ TAKE A SIP AND TALK ABOUT WHAT YOU TASTE

After you've taken a sip, keep the wine in your mouth for a few seconds and think about how it tastes. What you are looking for here is whether or not you taste any sweetness, acidity, or bitterness.

[
Wino Buzzword
CLOYING: This word is used negatively for wines that are unpleasantly sweet.
]

SWEETNESS: Wines that taste sweet have residual sugar, which occurs when the yeast doesn't convert all of the sugar in the grape juice to alcohol. If there is no residual sugar, the wine will taste "dry" (not sweet). If a wine is slightly sweet, it is called "off-dry." Dry sparkling wines are called "brut."

DID YOU KNOW...Sweetness and fruitiness are often confused. Fruitiness refers to fruitlike aromas that you smell, whereas sweetness is a sensation on your tongue. A wine with fruity aromas can be totally dry.

ACIDITY: A wine's acidity comes from the leftover acid in a grape's pulp at the time of harvest. Most of a grape's acid gets converted to sugar in the ripening process, but a little leftover acid is critical to the "crisp," "tart," and "refreshing" taste of certain wines. A wine lacking acidity can taste as uninspiring as a soda that's lost its carbonation. The wino buzzword for this is "flabby."

BITTERNESS: Bitterness in wine comes from excessive tannins. If you've ever had an inexpensive Cab, you've probably experienced that pucker factor or "astringency," as winos like to call it.

While you're sipping your wine, you also want to consider the "mouthfeel" of the wine. Have you ever heard someone describe a wine as light-bodied and smooth like silk? They're talking about how the body and the texture of the wine feels in their mouth—hence the term mouthfeel.

BODY: You can describe a wine's body as light, medium, or full. Light-bodied wines are often likened to the weight of skim milk in your mouth, whereas full-bodied wines are likened to the weight of heavy cream. If you paused at this comparison, read it again, this time focusing on the weight of the milk in your mouth instead of its taste or texture.

TEXTURE: The texture of a wine is often compared to fabrics. Wine can taste smooth like silk, soft like velvet, or rough like wool.

The Three Stages of a Taste of Wine

STAGE 1
the attack
When the wine first hits your tongue

STAGE 2
the mid-palate
When the wine is in your mouth on your tongue

STAGE 3
the finish
How long the flavors linger

SCRUTINIZE ▶ HERE'S WHERE YOU EXPLAIN WHY YOU'VE DECLARED A WINE "YUM" OR "YUCK"

It's easy to taste a wine and decide whether it's yum or yuck, but can you tell someone *why*? How about why a great wine is better than a good wine? Jennifer Simonetti-Bryan says there are three things that separate a great wine from a good wine:

1. Complexity 2. Balance 3. Length

Here are some questions that'll help you decide whether a wine is something special:

Q: DOES THE WINE HAVE A LOT TO SAY TO YOU?

Wines with "complex" aromas are considered higher quality because their many aromas make it easy for us to discuss the wine. Simonetti-Bryan says, "Simple wines are like a scoop of vanilla ice cream and complex wines are like ice-cream sundaes, with layers of Hershey's chocolate syrup, cherries, and peanuts."

Q: ARE THE FLAVORS INTEGRATED IN THE WINE? OR DO CERTAIN FLAVORS, TASTES, OR TEXTURES STICK OUT?

Karen MacNeil, author of *The Wine Bible,* describes an out-of-balance wine as a pointy star in the mouth that jabs the tongue with unpleasantness. For example, if a wine's acidity is out of balance, it will taste sour. If the tannins are out of balance, it will taste bitter. And if the alcohol is out of balance, it will taste "hot" on the palate. A "balanced" wine, on the other hand, is like a sphere in the mouth, where the flavors, acidity, tannins, and alcohol are in delicious, harmonious balance.

Q: DOES THE AFTERTASTE LINGER?

Or do the flavors stop immediately on your tongue? Wines with a longer "length" are considered higher quality. When you taste a wine, think about describing the length as long or short.

If the concept of balance seems difficult to grasp, it's because a wine's balance is somewhat subjective. A sommelier once told me, "Balance is in the eye of the beholder. While one person may think a wine is balanced wine, another person may disagree." If you think a wine tastes wonderfully integrated, then it did, regardless if someone else disagrees. The same way no one can tell you what paintings are beautiful, no one can tell you what wines you'll find beautifully balanced.

As you set out to develop your palate, don't take the five *s*'s too seriously. The goal is to have fun with it. Don't stress if the next time you pour yourself a glass you find it doesn't have a lot to say. Sometimes when I taste a wine, I conclude the wine smells like, well, *wine*.

To help with the fun part, I created a quick five *s*'s tasting shortcut for you. For easy access, find this cheat sheet on the Savvy Girl website and pin it to Pinterest so you've got it handy for your next wine-tasting adventure.

A SWEET TASTING SHORTCUT FOR THE SAVVY GIRL

Swirl & Smell

FRUIT		EARTH	WINEMAKING
WHITE WINES	**RED WINES**	O grass	O oak
O citrus fruits	O red berries	O forest floor	O vanilla
O stone fruits	O blackberries	O minerals	O toast
O apples	O plums	O flowers	

Sip

BODY	TASTE		TEXTURE
O light	O sweet	O crisp	O smooth
O medium	O off-dry	O tart	O soft
O full	O dry	O creamy	O tannic

Yum or Yuck?

O Does the taste linger?
O Did the wine have a lot to say?
O Was the wine a harmonious sphere of flavors or a pointy star?

YUM
O You are already pouring yourself another glass.

YUCK
O You'll bring a bottle to your frenemy's house the next time she hosts

Next Up

➔ Did you know that Champagne is a region in France—not a type of wine?

➔ What is the difference between a Sauvignon Blanc and a Chardonnay?

➔ Learn the buzzwords for your favorite white wines so you'll know how to describe them next time you ask for a wine recommendation.

Meet the A-list White Grapes

It was my friend's twenty-fourth birthday and she asked her girlfriends to join her on a wine-tasting getaway to the Santa Ynez wine region of California. Since she was entering her mid-twenties, she figured wine tasting was a more "sophisticated" way to get drunk on her birthday.

The first winery we hit had an outside tasting area surrounded by trellises overflowing with purple wisteria in full bloom. As we circled around the tasting bar and grabbed our wineglasses, we tried our best to pretend to know (and care) about wine.

That didn't last long.

By the time we got to the second winery, we forgot about our mid-twenties sophistication and instead of swirling and sipping we were cajoling the poor guy behind the counter into giving us extra pours. Although none of us really remember the third winery we went to that day, I'm pretty positive we made a quite a scene between all of the singing and endless photo ops.

One thing I do remember is buying several bottles of bubbly at our third stop. You know, because we were so classy. As we triumphantly boarded our party bus shouting, "Pop the Champagne!" our driver—understandably a little annoyed by then—lectured us on how we should be calling our California "Champagne" sparkling wine, because only sparkling wines from the Champagne region of France can be called Champagne.

Getting schooled by our party-bus driver was my first introduction to how wines can also be named after the region where the grapes were grown.

NEW WORLD VERSUS OLD WORLD WINE NAMES

In most Old World countries (think Europe), wines are named after the place the grapes were grown instead of by the name of the grape (for example, white Burgundy instead of Chardonnay) or by the type of wine (for example, Champagne instead of sparkling wine).

The reason Old World countries name their wines after the region instead of the varietal is deeply rooted in their winemaking history. Old World winemakers, who learned to make wine through generations of trial and error, discovered that certain grapes grew best in certain locations. The terroir, it seemed, had more of an influence on how the resulting wine would taste than merely the type of grape used to make the wine.

New World countries (think everywhere but Europe) believe that a wine's aromas are primarily influenced by the grape varietal. So, a Chardonnay will have the word "Chardonnay" on the label, regardless

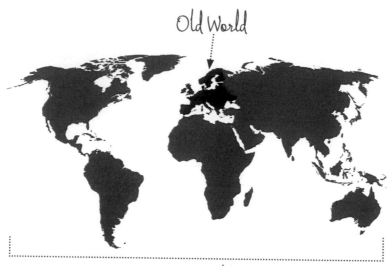

Old World

New World

of whether it's from New Zealand or Napa. The funny thing is, some French wine exporters have begun putting the varietal on their labels, since most Americans don't know what "Burgundy" means (Bourgogne, in French).

One other thing you need to know about Old World versus New World wines is that New World countries, in general, have a warmer climate in comparison to Old World countries. A warmer climate creates riper grapes, and riper grapes tend to make more full-bodied, fruit-forward wines.

Although warmer climates tend to make bolder wines, many Europeans say it takes a sophisticated palate to appreciate the subtleties and complexities of their wines. As you explore wines from other countries, you'll start to recognize this generalized difference in taste between Old World and New World wines. Whether you prefer bold New World wines or subtle Old World wines will depend on whatever is yum or yuck to you . . . or, as my best friend says, "yum or yummier."

THE BIG 8

Did you know that there are thousands of unique varieties of grapes? If you thought deciding between a Pinot Grigio and a Chardonnay was hard, just imagine if all several thousand varietals were made into wine. Even though there are more types of grapes than we could ever remember, only a few hundred are used to make wine—and even fewer are mass-produced enough to make it onto the shelves of your local liquor store.

Luckily, most of the wine you will encounter will be one of the Big 8—what I consider the eight most famous grape varietals. These A-lister grapes achieved their celeb status—or what winos call "noble" status—because they taste delicious and they grow well in a variety of terroirs.

The Big 8
Sauvignon Blanc
Chardonnay
Pinot Gris/Pinot Grigio
Riesling
Pinot Noir
Merlot
Cabernet Sauvignon
Syrah/Shiraz

You'll meet the A-list white grapes now, and in the next chapter you'll meet the A-list red grapes.

THE A–LIST WHITE GRAPES

MEET SAUVIGNON BLANC ▸ THE SASSY GRAPE

TYPICAL AROMA BUZZWORDS
Citrus fruits (grapefruit, lemon, lime), grass, minerals

TYPICAL TASTE BUZZWORDS
Dry, light-bodied, crisp, refreshing, acidic, tart

OLD WORLD SAUVIGNON BLANC ALIAS
Sancerre (France), Pouilly-Fumé (France),
White Bordeaux (France)

No white wine gets more bizarre descriptions than a Sauvignon Blanc. From "cat pee" to "herbaceous," these words can be put-downs or compliments, the same way "stinky" is a both praise and criticism for blue cheese.

Sauvignon Blanc, like blue cheese, has pungent aromas—it's a love it or hate it type of grape, and its high acidity, or tartness, will get your saliva glands going. The sassiness of a Sauvignon Blanc's acidity reminds me how one person may find a certain type of humor crude, while another person may find it totally refreshing and honest.

The first time I fell in love with Sauvignon Blanc I was living with a sorority sister who only drank New Zealand Sauvignon Blancs. It wasn't long before she started getting annoyed with how often I was "borrowing" her wines. What attracted me to these wines was their easily recognizable citrus aromas and refreshing taste, and for the first time I could actually describe why I thought a wine was a "yum."

A FUN FACT: Sauvignon Blanc grapes need to be grown in cool climates to preserve their refreshing acidity. Although the cool Marlborough region of New Zealand has stolen the spotlight, the northern Loire Valley of France is where the grape originated. French Sauvignon Blancs still have the same "sass in a glass" as New Zealand Sauvignon Blancs, but they are lighter in style and more minerally than citrusy.

MEET PINOT GRIS/PINOT GRIGIO ▸
THE GIRL-NEXT-DOOR GRAPE

TYPICAL AROMA BUZZWORDS:

Pears, peaches, floral, spice

TYPICAL TASTE BUZZWORDS:

Dry to off-dry, medium body, low to medium acidity

OLD WORLD PINOT GRIGIO/PINOT GRIS ALIAS:

Pinot Grigio (Italian name for the grape)

Pinot Gris (French name for the grape)

I've always thought Pinot Gris and Pinot Grigio (different names for the same grape) were a bit of a snooze fest. It's not that this wine tastes bad; it's just that it tastes uninteresting to me. This wine's lack of personality comes from its mild fruit aromas and mellow taste, which is probably what makes Pinot Grigio so popular; it's known for its "drinkability" (wine-speak for "goes down the hatch easily"). Like the proverbial girl next door, this wine gives us nothing to hate—no overt acidity, no odd aromas, and no heavy oak.

Despite my lack of enthusiasm for this grape, I recently bought an Oregon Pinot Gris and cracked it open with some Thai takeout. A couple bites of my spicy green papaya salad followed by a sip of that Oregon Pinot Gris and I finally understood why people drink this wine—it pairs nicely with food, especially food with a kick of spice.

The golden rule of food and wine pairing is to make sure that neither the wine nor the food is overpowering the other or competing with each other. Since a Pinot Grigio won't overpower even the mildest chicken noodle soup, its popularity is boosted by its success at the dinner table.

A FUN FACT: Although Pinot Gris and Pinot Grigio is the same grape, sometimes the different names are used to reference different styles when turned into wine. For example, Pinot Gris (the French style) is generally considered to have more body and spice than the lighter and fruitier Pinot Grigio (the Italian style).

MEET CHARDONNAY ▸ THE RUNWAY-MODEL GRAPE

TYPICAL AROMA BUZZWORDS
Apple, pear, sometimes minerals or tropical fruits
TYPICAL TASTE BUZZWORDS:
Dry, full-bodied, buttery (if oaked), and crisp (if unoaked)
OLD WORLD CHARDONNAY ALIAS:
White Burgundy (France); Pouilly-Fuissé (France); Chablis (France)

I like to think of Chardonnays like runway models. Most models walking down catwalks are beautiful, but in a subdued way. After all, they're hired to display a designer's work—and the designer's work is meant to be the focus, not the model. A Chardonnay is similar in that the wine from these grapes often has subdued aromas, making it the perfect wine for a winemaker to "dress up" in whatever style he or she chooses. These "dressed-up" styles include:

OAK AGING: Ever taste a toasty Chard? That's the product of the wine being aged in oak. Oak barrels are toasted (via fire) on the inside to adjust the flavors that will eventually be imparted to the wine. It's kind of like how a marshmallow can be just-barely toasted, browned all over, or roasted until it becomes a little fireball. Lightly toasted oak barrels impart vanilla and caramel flavors, while heavy-toasted oak barrels impart flavors such as cloves, cinnamon, smoke, or coffee.

LEES AGING: Sometimes a winemaker will age the wine on its lees, which are the combination of dead yeast cells and small

grape particles. Usually the lees are removed after fermentation, but extending their contact time with the wine boosts texture (creaminess) and flavor (nutty aromas).

MALOLACTIC FERMENTATION: The winemaker can also encourage a Chardonnay to go through malolactic fermentation (the cool kids call it "ML" or "Malo" for short). This process is routine for red wines but is a stylistic choice for white wines. This process turns the malic acid in wine (think of the acid in a tart green apple) to lactic acid (think of the softer acid in milk), which creates buttery aromas and creamy textures. In fact, one of the byproducts of ML is a chemical (diacetyl) that smells like melted butter.

Although a winemaker can dress up Chardonnay several ways, the new trend when it comes to Chardonnays is to go for a more "au naturel" style by using less oak or no oak at all. These lighter, not-so-oaky Chards are often called "naked" or "unwooded."

David Ramey, founder of and winemaker at Ramey Wine Cellars in Sonoma, California, makes one of my favorite Chardonnays. Ramey says that people have this unoaked trend all wrong. "The answer is not to throw out the barrels," he says. "Instead, the answer is to use oak judiciously." Ramey equates over-oaked Chards to oversalted foods. "Instead of choosing to forego salt altogether, people should use the right level of salt."

A FUN FACT: Even though Chardonnay originated in France, California stole the Chardonnay spotlight at the **1976 Judgment of Paris**. The now famous Judgment of Paris was a blind tasting that pitted Burgundy Chards against California Chards, and the panel of judges—who consisted of the then highest-ranking French wine snobs—ranked the **1973 Chateau Montelena Chardonnay** (a Napa Valley Chard) the highest. Of course, the judges scoffed at the verdict, and one even demanded to have her ballot back. This event is what put Napa, California on the map.

MEET RIESLING ▸ THE TEACHER'S PET GRAPE

TYPICAL AROMA BUZZWORDS:
Stone fruits (peaches, apricots), minerals ("steely"), floral

TYPICAL TASTE BUZZWORDS:
Light body, typically sweet (but also made in a dry style), high acidity, low to medium alcohol

OLD WORLD RIESLING ALIAS:
Germany labels many of their Rieslings by the varietal, however some higher-end Rieslings will have regional names such as "Rheingau" or "Mosel"

This grape is the biggest goody-goody of the bunch—kind of like that girl in your high school who sat in the front of the class, always did the reading, and never missed an opportunity for extra credit.

You see, Riesling is the favorite grape of almost all sommeliers because it exemplifies everything a major wino loves about wine. Remember how vines need a little vineyard "stress" to thrive? Well, Little Miss Riesling performs best in poor, stony soil, and in cool climates where its yield is curbed (making fewer but juicer grapes). Riesling is also considered a highly aromatic wine, meaning its aromas have a lot to say—like the teacher's pet whose hand shoots up in the air after each question is asked.

You probably won't be surprised to hear that Rieslings also show off in the extra-credit category. For example, a Riesling's natural high acidity gives it the ability to be one of the only white wines that can age well over time. As a Riesling ages, it develops aromas of petrol (gasoline); aromas only a sommelier could love.

DID YOU KNOW...Rieslings are seldom aged in oak because the oaky flavors clash with this grape's aromas and acidity.

A FUN FACT: Rieslings come in two different styles: sweet or dry. The sweet style is what most people think of when they hear "Riesling." To make a Riesling sweet, the winemaker must stop the fermentation process before the yeast finishes converting all of the sugar into alcohol. This residual sugar creates a wine that tastes sweeter and is lower in alcohol.

Next Up

➜ Did you know that not all wines improve with age?

➜ What does "improve with age" mean, anyway?

➜ Learn the buzzwords for your favorite red wines so you'll know how to describe them next time you ask for a wine recommendation.

ch4

Meet the A-list Red grapes

It was a total shock when I first learned that not all wines improve with age.

It was right after college, and a close friend's grandfather had passed away. My friend helped his family clean out his grandfather's home and in the back of his grandfather's dusty pantry were several "old" bottles of red wine. My friend figured he was in for a real treat and he graciously shared one of these bottles with me. Let's just say we were a little disappointed when we opened the bottle. We didn't even need to taste the wine to know it had gone bad. One whiff of sour vinegar and we knew.

Turns out that 95 percent of all wine is made to be consumed within a year, so my friend's grandfather's wine was either fifteen years past its prime or it had been stored improperly for far too long.

Even if you do buy a bottle that can improve with age, why wait?

HOW A WINE IMPROVES WITH AGE

I got the answer to this question when I tasted two high-end red wines side by side at my local wine shop. The first wine was a "young" wine that had been bottled only a month prior to us popping its cork. The second wine was an "old" wine that had been bottle-aged for twelve years.

The shop owner first poured me a taste of the young wine. What surprised me most was how the fruit and oak flavors tasted totally separate. As I took a sip, I tasted fresh, ripe fruit flavors, and then I tasted oak flavors. It was as if the fruit and the oak weren't talking to each other.

When I made these comments about the young wine, the wine shop owners looked at each other, gave a nod, and poured me a small sip of the old wine, a super-spendy and highly sought-after red wine. Remember what I told you about how people will share nice wine with you if they think you can "appreciate" it?

When I smelled the aged wine, its bottle-aged aromas (or "bouquet" in wine-speak) of leather, earth, and dried fruits were hypnotizing. Identifying those aromas, especially the leather aroma, was surprisingly not difficult after experiencing the freshness and fruitiness of the young wine.

Next, I took a sip of the old wine and instantly noticed the way the flavors tasted like one homogenous "round" taste—like the "perfect sphere" Karen MacNeil said you get from a balanced wine. When I sipped that aged red wine, it was impossible to tell where one flavor ended and another began. Twelve years of bottle aging had allowed the wine's fruit, oak, and tannin to meld into one another the same way the ingredients in a stew blend together after hours of simmering.

While that tasting experience perfectly illustrated how a wine can improve with age, I concluded that, at least for now, I am too impatient to wait more than a decade to enjoy a wine. Instead, the amount of bottle aging I will be doing will consist of the time it takes to get the wine from the store and into my glass.

That being said, in case you have a wine cellar (and a lot more patience than I do), it's good to know which wines have the potential to get better with age. The cheat sheet answer: Reds. So, let's meet these age-worthy A-lister red grapes.

savvy tip
> If you do buy a bottle you want to age, make sure it's from a good producer, a good vintage, and that it's a premium wine. Inexpensive reds from the liquor store are not designed to age well. If you are going to spend the money but you're not sure if the wine has what it takes to improve over time, ask the storeowner.

THE A-LIST RED GRAPES

MEET PINOT NOIR ▸ THE SEXY DIVA GRAPE

TYPICAL AROMA BUZZWORDS:

Cherries, sour cherries, strawberries, earth

TYPICAL TASTE BUZZWORDS:

Dry, light-bodied, smooth/silky texture

OLD WORLD PINOT NOIR ALIAS:

Red Burgundy (France)

Madeline Triffon, the ninth American to earn the title of Master Sommelier, once called Pinot Noir "sex in a glass" because of its intoxicating aromas and smooth taste. Whenever I drink Pinot Noir, I'm reminded of my hot fling with a sexy French guy I met the summer after college. All it takes is one sip of Pinot Noir's soft and supple texture and I am lost in the memory of clutching his sculpted abs while riding on the back of his motorcycle.

The soft, smooth, "sexy" nature of a Pinot Noir comes from the grape's low tannin levels. Some people assume that since Pinot Noirs are more transparent in color and lighter in body, their flavors will be equally thin. However, the contrast of a Pinot Noir's complex flavors yet light body presents itself gracefully on the palate, the way a French person makes pronouncing French words sound effortless.

Loving Pinot Noir also takes the type of sophistication you get through experience. It's like graduating from Mike's Hard Lemonade to a dirty martini. When I first ventured beyond Cabernet Sauvignon (my original go-to red) I hated Pinot Noir. That was because I expected a big, bold, tannic Cabernet Sauvignon. When I searched for the tannins, I thought it tasted diluted. (I'm thinking I might have had a bottom-shelf Pinot).

A FUN FACT: Pinot Noir is infamous for being difficult to grow; it's a temperamental and high-maintenance grape. Pinot Noir's thin skins make the grape susceptible to damage from the sun, wind, frost, and disease, resulting in a lot of bad batches. Translation? Be prepared to pay up for a quality Pinot Noir.

MEET MERLOT ▸ THE INTROVERTED GRAPE

TYPICAL AROMA BUZZWORDS:

Plums, blackberries

TYPICAL TASTE BUZZWORDS:

Dry, medium body, low acidity, soft tannins, moderate oak

OLD WORLD MERLOT ALIAS:

(Right Bank) Bordeaux (France)

The British wine critic Oz Clarke once described Merlot as the eternal bridesmaid to Cabernet Sauvignon. That might be a little harsh, but the truth is that sometimes Merlots can be a bit of a dud since they lack the attention-grabbing tannins of a Cab or the intense aromas of a Pinot Noir.

However, whatever Merlot may lack in personality, it makes up for in its famous plush and velvety-soft taste. One sip of Merlot's softness can be as comforting as snuggling with your favorite pillow. If Pinot Noirs are soft and silky, Merlots are soft and juicy, with ripe plum and blackberry flavors.

To make Merlot less of a wallflower, it is often blended with other varietals, such as Cab Franc or Cabernet Sauvignon, which boosts a Merlot's flavor and intensity. But before you conclude that this is another example of how Merlot is stuck in Cabernet Sauvignon's shadow, know that Cabernet Sauvignon is often blended with a bit of Merlot to soften the harshness of its tannins.

A FUN FACT: Some of the most expensive wines are Merlots. For example, Pétrus, the most famous Merlot in the world (from the Bordeaux region of France), goes for $3,000 a bottle. If $3K per bottle isn't exactly your style (in other words, you aren't royalty), the good news is that Merlot is one of the easier grapes to grow. Translation? There are more affordable quality Merlots than there are Pinot Noirs or Cabernet Sauvignons.

MEET CABERNET SAUVIGNON ▸ THE SUPERMODEL GRAPE

TYPICAL AROMA BUZZWORDS:

Black currant, cassis, blackberries

TYPICAL TASTE BUZZWORDS:

Dry, full-bodied, medium to high acidity, bold flavors, oaky, tannic

OLD WORLD CABERNET SAUVIGNON ALIAS:

(Left Bank) Bordeaux (France)

Cabernet Sauvignon, or Cab for short, is famous for its distinctive black currant or cassis aromas (cassis is another name for currant, and crème de cassis is a liqueur made from black currants). If you are wondering what the heck a black currant is, you are not alone. Black currants aren't common in the United States, so it took me months of searching before I finally found some in a gourmet food market. Turns out they taste a lot like blackberries.

Cabernet Sauvignon is often called the Chardonnay of red wines, except Cabs are bigger, bolder, and sexier. If Chardonnays are like runway models, Cabs are like the breakout supermodel whose career extends beyond the runway—think Heidi Klum or Tyra Banks.

Cabernet Sauvignon's famous bold and robust flavor profile is a result of the grapes' thick skins and small berries. The thick skins are responsible for the high tannin levels in a Cab, and they also act as a preservative, giving this wine major aging potential.

In a Cabernet Sauvignon's youth these tannins bring a "fierceness" to the wine, the same way Heidi and Tyra brought attitude to the catwalk. As Heidi and Tyra seem to only get more successful with time, Cabernet Sauvignon also excels in the maturation period, where oak-barrel aging and time in the bottle allow the tannins to soften and the flavors to integrate, creating a better, more refined wine.

A FUN FACT: Remember the 1976 Judgment of Paris and how the Chateau Montelena Chardonnay from Napa beat out the French wine? Well, in the Cabernet Sauvignon category, a California wine also won. The winner? The 1973 Stag's Leap Wine Cellars Cabernet Sauvignon from Napa Valley.

MEET SYRAH/SHIRAZ ▶ THE CHAMELEON GRAPE

TYPICAL AROMA BUZZWORDS:
Raspberry, blackberry, black pepper, grilled meats
TYPICAL TASTE BUZZWORDS:
Dry, full-bodied, rich, luscious fruit
OLD WORLD SYRAH ALIAS:
(Northern) Côtes du Rhône (France); Shiraz (Australia)

First things first: Syrah and Shiraz is actually the same grape. The only difference is that Australia calls their wines made from the Syrah grape "Shiraz." Also, Petite Sirah is a totally different grape from Syrah, and there is nothing "petite" about its taste. In fact, Petite Sirah is so brawny and tough to drink that most Petite Sirahs need to have other wines blended in to make the wine drinkable. Years of confusion cleared up in one go, am I right?

The next thing you need to know about Syrah is that this grape is a total chameleon.

According to Ryan Hill, fourth generation of the Hill Family Estate in Napa, whose family makes a Syrah wine, "Syrah can grow anywhere and everywhere." Since this grape can grow in a variety of terroirs, it has the ability to show a sense of place in its flavors. For example, an Australian Shiraz is known for obvious fruit and "jammy" aromas, while a cooler climate Syrah has primary flavors of spice and pepper and more subtle fruit flavors. If you like Syrahs, this knowledge will help you choose one style over another at a restaurant.

The Hill family in Napa makes one of my favorite Syrahs. I asked Hill what makes his family's Syrah so special, and he told me that in order to get depth and concentration, Syrah needs to ripen slowly. "The combination of a cool and windy vineyard location and using new oak [during maturation] allows our Syrah to have the fruit, smoke, and intensity needed to give it that Syrah charm," he says.

A FUN FACT: The bolder fruit style of the Australian Shiraz has become so popular (despite wine snobs calling them fruit bombs) that some countries who also have warmer climates now call their Syrahs Shiraz, to indicate their wine is made in the Australian bold fruit style.

Next Up

➜ Have you ever felt nervous asking for help at a wine shop? Keep reading for tips on how to ask for a recommendation.

➜ Should you care whether 2012 was better than 2011 when you buy wine?

➜ What does a "92 point" wine rating actually mean? And who does the rating?

How to buy Wine

Before I knew much about wine, my typical wine-buying experience looked like this: I would aimlessly wander the wine aisles for far too long trying to find the "perfect" bottle of wine. The minutes would pass and I'd quickly become frustrated at the overwhelming number of choices. Out of desperation—and because my frozen goods were starting to thaw—I would settle on a bottle with a cute animal label, hoping the cuteness would alleviate my fear of missing out on a better wine.

Then, as soon as I decided I was pleased with my choice, I would spot another interesting wine with a slightly higher price tag and an even cuter label. Holding both bottles and standing there like an idiot, I would question whether the more expensive wine was *way* better than the cheaper one I'd initially chosen.

The more time I'd spend in the wine aisle, the more time my FOMO—fear of missing out—would steer me toward the more expensive bottle, and then I'd justify my choice with the cliché "You get what you pay for."

If only wine were that simple—if each extra dollar spent guaranteed extra-delicious wine—maybe I'd have wasted less time wandering the wine aisles. But the beauty of wine, especially for us semi-broke Savvy Girls, is that enjoying delicious vino doesn't require a big budget. It all comes back to whatever you think is yum or yuck. And trust me, finding a fabulous inexpensive bottle feels every bit as victorious as snagging a designer bag for half off.

PRICE AND QUALITY ▸ WHAT THE PRICE CAN TELL YOU ABOUT A WINE

How can a wine cost as little as $4.99 and as much as $50 (or more)?

A higher price isn't just a needless markup for more profit. When a winery prices their wine, what they charge reflects the costs incurred in making that wine—things like owning land, barrel aging, and even factors such as marketing and distribution. Higher-quality wines, in general, cost more money to make, although it is definitely not a one-to-one correlation. Things like famous winemakers, well-known regions, and positive reviews from industry movers and shakers can add plenty of "brand equity" to the price tag.

THREE FACTORS THAT CONTRIBUTE TO THE PRICE OF WINE

1. THE REAL ESTATE AND BRAND EQUITY

Want a *Grand Cru* red Burgundy (read: the cream of the crop Pinot Noir from France)? Expect to pay up. Burgundy real estate is about as expensive and elite as penthouses on the island of Manhattan. Like the price of an apartment overlooking Central Park, the limited number of wines made from the elite vineyards of Burgundy mean those wineries have to charge top dollar to cover their costs. What's more, Burgundy wines also benefit from name recognition, so these wineries can demand a higher premium the same way Christian Louboutin can charge $1,000 for a pair of his famous red-soled shoes.

If you're looking for value, explore wines from less famous New World wine regions, such as Chile.

2. AGING IN OAK BARRELS

If a winemaker chooses to make a wine in an oaked style, she's got to fork over serious dollars for those oak barrels—especially French oak. Remember: French oak has a tighter grain and fewer knots than American oak, so the wood splits straight when being made into barrels. "Since French oak has a straighter grain than American oak, less of the cell walls are cut, and the wood imparts less aggressive tannins into the wine," says Peter Smith, a contributor to the *Sommelier Journal.*

This is why a Cabernet Sauvignon aged in French oak barrels is typically more expensive than Cabernet Sauvignon aged in American oak barrels, and why oaked wines in general are pricier than wines that are aged in stainless steel.

3. WEATHER

Wine is essentially an agricultural product that is dictated by Mother Nature. This means the years with good weather yield more grapes, and the years with bad weather yield fewer grapes. I spoke with a sales and production manager at a major winery and he told me that one case of wine costs the same to make regardless of the level of production. That means the price of a bottle of wine can increase in bad-weather years.

WHERE TO BUY WINE AND HOW TO ASK FOR HELP

Have you ever bought a blouse online and when it arrived, you discovered it didn't look the same as it did online? Buying wine without tasting it first reminds me of the majority of my online purchases—most don't live up to my expectations.

These days I do a lot of my wine buying at wine shops where I can "try before I buy"—or at least where I can chat with someone about what's in the bottle.

My favorite place to buy wine is at any **boutique wine shop**. Most towns have these shops, and they typically offer weekly wine tastings, where you can try several wines for around $10. Since wine labels are about as helpful as a 105-pound, five-foot-eleven girl modeling a blouse, the "try before you buy" concept is an awesome way to discover new wines and bring home winners each time.

Christopher Hennessy, a sommelier in Los Angeles, says shopping at a wine boutique is a low-pressure experience because the storeowners are typically eager to help you. "At a small wine shop, there's no need to pretend that you know more than you do about wine," says Hennessy. "These people absolutely love guiding their customers in the right direction—it's what keeps shoppers coming back to their store."

HOW TO TELL A WINE MERCHANT WHAT YOU WANT

Even though Hennessy says you don't need to fake your wine knowledge, showing up and asking someone to recommend "something yummy" probably won't help you walk out with a wine you'll love.

Before we get to the best way to ask for a recommendation, let's start with what *not* to ask.

WHAT NOT TO ASK WHEN BUYING WINE

CAN YOU RECOMMEND A "GOOD" WINE? This is vague. It's like going to Bloomingdale's and asking the salesgirl to help you find a cute dress.

What does "cute" mean to you? And are you looking for a dress to wear to work or on a third date?

DO YOU HAVE A NICE, FRUITY WINE? This is also vague. It's like asking that same salesgirl for a "feminine" dress. All wines have fruit aromas, but the fruit aromas can come in different styles. Try telling the shop owner what kind of fruits you like, such as citrus fruits, cherries, or rich, jamlike fruits. If you prefer wines with strong fruit aromas, say "fruit-forward" instead of "fruity."

WHAT IS THE MOST HIGHLY RATED WINE YOU HAVE? Lots of people and wine magazines do ratings, and who knows whether the person doing the rating has the same palate as you do. Plus, here's a little secret: The price of wine often skyrockets after it receives a superior rating.

WHAT TO ASK WHEN BUYING WINE

Paddy Delepine, the owner of Bacchus Wine Made Simple, a boutique wine shop in Manhattan Beach, California, says the more details you can give someone, the better. "Ideally, we want to know the types of wine you like, the occasion, and what your price range is," says Delepine. She also wants people to know they don't need to worry about saying the *right* things to her when asking about wine. As long as her customers try to describe what they are looking for, she says she can usually figure out what they want.

For example, one time a customer asked Delepine for an "oaky, buttery, red wine." The term "buttery" is used more extensively to describe white wines (usually Chardonnays) with a rich, creamy texture and a smooth finish similar to liquid butter. So, Delepine asked her customer a few more questions and was able to conclude that this "buttery" quality her customer wanted was probably a red wine with a soft taste and a smooth finish, such as a Merlot or a Pinot Noir.

"Customers should never be intimidated just because they might not know the perfect wine terminology," says Delepine. "They just know what they like. It's our job to ask more questions and interpret what those answers mean."

Now that you know you can ask for help without being judged, here are some guidelines on what to tell someone like Delepine when you're shopping for wine:

YOUR BUDGET: Wine-shop owners spend a lot of time curating their selection, which means they've tried most of their wines—if not all of them—and they know which $10 bottle tastes like a $30 bottle.

WHY YOU'RE BUYING THE WINE: The recommendation will be different if you're going to a friend's BBQ versus cooking pumpkin risotto for a romantic dinner.

WHAT YOU LIKE OR DON'T LIKE IN A WINE: Now that you're more fluent in wine-speak, you've got the buzzwords to explain what's yum or yuck to you. If you are still learning what you do and don't like in a wine, mention the name of a wine you recently loved. Chances are the wine shop worker may have heard of it and can recommend a similar wine.

savvy tip [Ever tried a wine you love and wanted to buy it again? Use the website www.wine-searcher.com to locate the nearest wine store to you that carries it.]

WINE-OF-THE-MONTH CLUBS

For anywhere from $30 to $100 a month, wine clubs will send you two or more bottles of wine, delivered to your door. In the past, I belonged to a few wine-of-the-month clubs, and after many months of auto-payments and random wines, I finally got sick of pouring nine out of ten of them down the drain. It's not that I am especially picky; I just found most of the wines I received undrinkable. (So undrinkable that I didn't even feel like I could offload them at a party.)

Christopher Hennessy says these "wine-of-the-month" type of deals have received a bad reputation in the last few years because the wine you get is frequently low quality. "When the consumer guarantees they will pay $40 a month for two bottles of wine, many companies have a hard time resisting sending wine they can get for $5 a bottle—and then pocketing the rest as profit," says Hennessy.

But not all wine clubs are bad. Many wineries have their own wine clubs, where you can get quarterly shipments of their wines. Going direct to your favorite winery is a great way to get discounts. The only downside to this is that you'd better want to drink the same wine all the time.

Some newer wine-of-the-month clubs, such as **Club W,** ask their customers to take a palate-profile quiz when they sign up. Questions like, "How do you take your coffee?" and "Do you like orange juice?" help them understand your affinity for bitterness and acidity in a wine. Club W cofounder Geoffrey McFarlane says they created the palate profile quiz because "most people don't know what wines they like, but they do know what foods they like; since what we like in food is relatable to what we will like in wine, it helps us make appropriate wine recommendations for our members."

HOW TO READ A WINE LABEL

You won't always have a friendly shop owner or a cool palate-profile quiz to point you in the right direction. Sometimes all you'll have to go on is the label, and that is why there are so many cute critter labels—wine marketers know that when we are confused, some of us look for something with an adorable animal on it.

Unfortunately, knowing how to read the label won't guarantee you'll always buy a bottle you'll love, but at least it'll help you look like less of a tourist in the wine aisle.

NEW WORLD WINE LABELS

For the most part, New World wine labels (the United States, Australia, New Zealand, Chile, and so on) include the producer of the wine, the varietal, the vintage, the alcohol-by-volume level (ABV), and where the grapes were grown (the appellation).

producer ──────▶ **CARMEL ROAD**   *alcohol content*

region or appellation ──────▶ MONTEREY

ALC. 13.5% VOL

varietal ──────▶ CHARDONNAY | CERTIFIED SUSTAINABLE

ARROYO SECO, MONTEREY *vintage* 2011 ◀────── *vintage*

PRODUCER

Not all wineries make and produce their wine. If you see "Estate Bottled" on the label, it means the winery also grew the grapes. Many wineries buy grapes from other producers. For example, The Hill Family Estate winery in Napa sells 80 percent of the grapes they grow to other winemakers (including Silver Oak, Caymus, Stag's Leap, Cakebread, and Quintessa).

VARIETAL

The use of a varietal name on a label is a regulated term. As long as 75 percent of the wine is made from the varietal listed on the bottle, the winery can name the wine by the varietal. This means the wine could have up to 25 percent of some mystery grape (a tactic used to keep production costs down, considering no-name grapes will be cheaper than, say, Riesling or Chardonnay grapes). If the winery names what other grapes they have blended into the wine, then the blending was done to enhance the taste of the wine and they are probably proud of it.

THE VINTAGE

The vintage, or the year on the label, is the year the grapes were harvested. But don't worry, you don't need to have a vintage chart in your pocket or care whether 2011 was a better year than 2012. Remember, the majority of wines you can buy at the store are meant to be consumed right away, so you want to make sure the wine isn't too old. If you see a five-year-old Sauvignon Blanc or two-year-old Beaujolais Nouveau, skip 'em and move on.

ALCOHOL CONTENT (AKA ABV)

When I was first buying wine, I thought the more alcohol in the bottle, the better. Why would I let them gyp me out of booze? But that was before I learned that the alcohol-by-volume content gives clues about the style and quality of the wine. For example, normal ABV levels are between 12 and 14 percent for wine, and this usually indicates a medium-bodied wine. A lower ABV (less than 12 percent) usually indicates a lighter-bodied wine, and one that may have a higher residual sugar level. Some high-alcohol wines can taste "hot" on the palate, so if you have nothing else to go on, look for an alcohol content at 14 percent and lower.

REGION/APPELLATION

Appellation is a fancy word for "land," and it means regulated grape-growing areas within each state or region. Appellations in the United States, such as Napa, Finger Lakes, or Willamette Valley, are registered with the US government and are referred to as American

Viticulture Areas (or AVAs).

To put a registered AVA (such as Napa Valley) on a label, 85 percent of the wine in the bottle must have been grown in that appellation. This is so a winery can't put Napa Valley on the label if the grapes weren't grown there.

The reason this matters comes back to terroir. The better the terroir, the better the grapes; the better the grapes, the better the wine. For example, Cabernet Sauvignon from the appellation of Napa Valley is likely a higher quality wine than a Cabernet Sauvignon from the appellation of California, which is vague and means the grapes could've been grown on the side of Interstate 5.

There are a lot of appellation names for each wine region; Napa Valley alone has sixteen sub-AVAs, such as "St. Helena" or "Rutherford." At the most basic level, just know this: Appellations guarantee where the grapes were grown, and the more specific the appellation, often the higher the quality of the wine.

Wine Label Buzzwords to Know

CUVÉE: Think "blend" when you see this term. "Cuvée" is a French word that means "blended batch of wines," usually used to describe Champagnes. When you see this on a wine label, it indicates the wine is either a blend of wines from several vineyards or a blend of varietals.

MERITAGE: This word rhymes with "heritage" (so if you say "merry taj" you're pronouncing it wrong), and it's a word created by California winemakers who want to indicate their wine is made in a Bordeaux style. Red wines from the Bordeaux region of France are usually a blend of either Cabernet Sauvignon, Merlot, or Cabernet Franc as the predominant grape. White wines from the Bordeaux region of France are usually a blend of Sauvignon Blanc, Sémillon and sometimes Muscadelle.

CLARET: This word has no regulated definition, but it usually refers to a Bordeaux-style red wine. This wine may come in a lighter style, since the original clarets were more of a cross between a red wine and a rosé.

Unregulated Words on Labels

RESERVE: The term "reserve" is unregulated in California. Some states, such as Washington, have stricter rules. For example, in Washington State only 10 percent of a winery's wines can be called reserve.

OLD VINE: The term "old vine" is typically seen on Zinfandel labels and is also unregulated. It is said that as vines grow older, they produce fewer but more concentrated grapes, making more flavorful wine. If you see this on a label, take it with a grain of salt.

OLD WORLD WINE LABELS

Old World wine labels contain similar information to what you'll find on a New World label—but they are *way* more confusing. Not only are the words often not in English, but remember most Old World wines are named after the region instead of the varietal. (Alsace, France, is one of the exceptions.)

To add to the confusion, the appellation system (the regulated grape-growing areas) in these Old World countries is about as clear and interesting as the US tax code. In France, their wine police— known as the Appellation d'Origine Contrôlée (or the AOC)— not only regulates the boundaries of their famous wine regions, but they've also made it illegal (yep, illegal) to plant varietals not already approved for these famous regions. Their wine police even regulate winemaking techniques, such as yield restrictions and aging techniques.

And if your eyes aren't starting to glaze over by now, they will if I dig into the French hierarchical appellation system. So instead, take a look at my cheat sheet that'll help you understand the most relevant part of an Old World wine label: Which regions equal which varietals. You're welcome.

France

FRANCE'S WINE POLICE = "AOC"

The best wines are classified as Grand Cru and only feature the vineyard name (for example, "Chambertin.")

(WHITE) BURGUNDY = CHARDONNAY

(RED) BURGUNDY = PINOT NOIR

The labels typically contain the names of the villages, vineyards, or subappellations. Ex.'s: Bourgogne (region) Meursault (village), Meursault-Perrières (village and vineyard)

(WHITE) BORDEAUX = A BLEND
MADE FROM SAUVIGNON BLANC AND/OR SÉMILLON, SOMETIMES MUSCADELLE

(RED) BORDEAUX = TYPICALLY A BLEND
EITHER PREDOMINANTLY MERLOT OR CABERNET SAUVIGNON

(WHITE) SANCERRE = SAUVIGNON BLANC

(RED) SANCERRE = PINOT NOIR

CHAMPAGNE = SPARKLING WINE
MADE FROM THE CHARDONNAY, PINOT NOIR AND PINOT MEUNIER VARIETALS

BEAUJOLAIS = GAMAY NOIR VARIETAL

RHÔNE = MOSTLY BLENDS
USUALLY HAVE GRENACHE (IN THE SOUTH), AND SYRAH (IN THE NORTH)

Châteauneuf-du-Pape is a famous Rhône Blend. (There are about 13 permitted grapes in this blend).

Italy

ITALY'S WINE POLICE= DOC OR DOCG

A term to describe the growing number of wines made to compete in the world with Bordeaux-style blends.

If you see "Classico" on the label it refers to a town in Chianti called Classico. The only distinguishing factor between Chianti Classico and Chianti Classico Riserva is the required aging.

CHIANTI = SANGIOVESE VARIETAL

SOAVE = GARGANEGA VARIETAL

BAROLO = NEBBIOLO VARIETAL

BARBARESCO = NEBBIOLO VARIETAL

SUPER TUSCAN = RED BLEND (BORDEAUX-STYLE)

BARBERA D'ASTI = BARBERA VARIETAL FROM ASTI

BARBERA D'ALBA = BARBERA VARIETAL FROM ALBA

MOSCATO D'ASTI = MOSCATO VARIETAL FROM ASTI

Many wines in the great northeast are varietal, such as Pinot Grigio and/or Prosecco (made from the Glera grape)

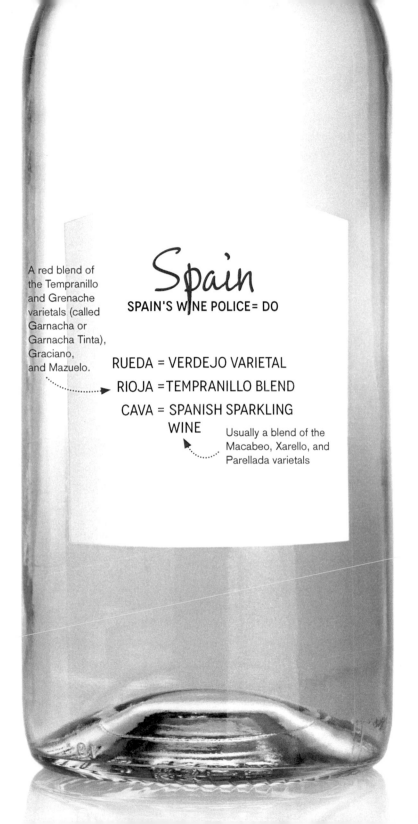

A red blend of the Tempranillo and Grenache varietals (called Garnacha or Garnacha Tinta), Graciano, and Mazuelo.

Spain

SPAIN'S WINE POLICE = DO

RUEDA = VERDEJO VARIETAL

RIOJA = TEMPRANILLO BLEND

CAVA = SPANISH SPARKLING WINE

Usually a blend of the Macabeo, Xarello, and Parellada varietals

THE WINE RATING SYSTEM ▸ 92 POINTS ACCORDING TO WHOM?

Have you ever had a hard time choosing a wine? Wine merchants know the answer to that question is yes. If you see a sticker that says "92 points," you're more likely to grab that bottle, thinking someone who knows more about wine than you do gave that wine a high score, right?

This is exactly why wine points exist. They bring some clarity to the sea of choices available to you by using a rating system everyone knows — the 100-point grading system from our school days.

Robert Parker, arguably the most famous wine critic, is credited for being the one who got everyone using the 100-point system. The scale starts at 50 points, with 100 points being the highest score and 50 being the lowest. Wines get points for different categories, including color, aroma, taste, finish, balance, and more.

Since wines that score an 88 or higher tend to sell like hotcakes, critics of this 100-point system argue that many Bordeaux producers now wait for Parker's ratings before setting the price of their wines. Some even claim that many wines are produced in a style that will please Parker's palate. (Where was this job on Career Day?)

The bottom line? Take wine ratings with a grain of salt. While a highly rated wine is probably pretty good, experts agree there's a hefty dose of bias and politics that play into these scores.

Next Up

➔ How to read a wine list.

➔ How to sound savvy when asking a sommelier for a wine recommendation.

➔ The wine-pouring ritual: What are you supposed to do with the cork? And when is it acceptable to send a wine back?

ch 6
Ordering wine at a Restaurant

Tell me if you've ever had this nightmare: It's the end of the semester, your final is on Monday, and somehow you've managed to go the entire semester without going to class. In fact, you didn't even know you were enrolled in that class.

This is kind of like how I used to feel when I was handed the wine list—you know, the ones that are so thick and heavy they look like a textbook. I would sift through thirty pages of wines I'd never heard of and I'd wonder if I had forgotten to show up to some "life" class where I was supposed to learn this stuff.

Usually by the time I hit the French wines section, and every other bottle was starting to sound like "Château de Blah-Blah," I would settle for a bottle that was a step up from the cheapest and something I was 99 percent confident I could pronounce. All the while hoping the sommelier wouldn't catch on to what I was doing.

If you can relate, keep reading. My goal is that when you finish this chapter, you'll be comfortable reaching for the wine list, asking a sommelier for a recommendation, and handling the wine-pouring ritual like you've been a front-row regular all semester.

ANATOMY OF A WINE LIST

In general, restaurants offer wines by the glass and wines by the bottle, although some will let you order half bottles or carafes.

Ordering by the glass is a good call if you want to try new varietals and wines from regions you haven't explored yet. Lisa Hemmat, sommelier and proprietor of Lido di Manhattan in Los Angeles (she was featured on Gordon Ramsay's restaurant makeover show, *Kitchen Nightmares*) tries to include a few unique varietals and blends in her by-the-glass wines to inspire her customers to try something new. For example, Lisa fell in love with the Cabernet Franc grape while getting her sommelier certification, so she always includes a Cab Franc by the glass on her wine list.

Ordering by the bottle is best when you are with your friends or family and everyone plans on having more than one glass of wine, since it's usually a better deal to order by the bottle as long as everyone is excited about drinking the same thing.

HOW A WINE LIST WORKS

All wine lists are different, of course, but they're usually organized in one of these four ways:

1. By varietal (Sauvignon Blanc, Merlot, etc.)
2. By geography (country, state, or region)
3. By style (dry, sweet, light and crisp, full-bodied and bold)
4. By price ($30 wines, $60 wines, $90 wines, etc.)

Regardless of how the wine list is organized, each list will include the varietal or place name (if it's an Old World wine), the producer, the appellation, and usually the vintage.

Wine List

producer | type | region

		glass | bottle
Fransiscan Cabernet, *Napa Valley*		11 | 35
Dynamite Cabernet, *North Coast*		8 | 25
Simi Cabernet, *Alexander Valley*		| 40
Stags Leap Artemis, *Napa Valley*		| 110
Rodney Strong, *Russian River*		| 30
Chalone Pinot noir, *Central Coast*		8 | 25

No matter how well versed you are in wine, the best way to order an awesome wine is to ask for help. Considering there are thousands of different wines out there and each year there are new vintages, chances are you probably haven't tried every wine on the menu.

You know who has tried every wine on the menu? The restaurant's sommelier. It's her job to create the wine list and help people like you choose something you'll love.

HERE'S HOW TO TALK TO A SOMMELIER WITHOUT FLS (FEAR OF LOOKING STUPID)

Once you engage a sommelier, she is going to ask you a bunch of questions. These questions aren't meant to expose your lack of wine knowledge, although it may feel that way. Instead, these questions are intended to help her make a recommendation that you'll love so much, you'll want to be a regular at that restaurant. Remember, your patronage keeps the restaurant in business, so the sommelier wants you to be happy.

Here's what the sommelier will ask....

1. WHAT ARE YOU PLANNING ON ORDERING?

Food and wine pairing is like choosing the right shoes for an outfit. They can go together perfectly and enhance each other—or they can clash as bad as a pencil skirt and sneakers. Your sommelier will want to know what you're eating so her wine recommendation will pair nicely with your food. Think of the sommelier like your personal stylist.

2. WHAT STYLE OF WINE DO YOU LIKE?

This is where you need to be thinking of those buzzwords you know: sweet or dry, crisp or smooth, light or full-bodied, and fruit-forward or earthy.

Each varietal comes in a range of styles, so your sommelier wants to make sure she steers you toward the right one. If you know you like crisp, light-bodied wines—but don't like wines with overly grassy aromas—let her know. If you are unsure what wines you like, Hemmat says to "tell your server what fruits you like, such as blackberries or raspberries, because this is enough information to help the sommelier make a wine recommendation."

Brian Smith, a sommelier who spent time at top restaurants in Las Vegas and New York City, agrees that you don't need to memorize poetic tasting notes to describe what you like. "The most important buzzword to know when describing the style of wine you like is 'body,' because it is the most basic differentiator," he says. "If you tell a sommelier you prefer full-bodied reds, that alone narrows a selection substantially."

3. WHAT REGIONS OR VARIETALS DO YOU LIKE? DO YOU WANT TO TRY SOMETHING NEW?

If you're not sure what style of wine you like or what you're in the mood for, tell the sommelier the varietal, producer, or region of wines you've liked in the past. Something along the lines of, "I prefer Merlots" or "I like Kendall Jackson Chardonnay," or even "I like Italian red wines" will help her make a better recommendation.

If I tell the sommelier I want to try something new, I make sure to let her know what I *don't* like so she can take that into account. For example, I've never met a Riesling I've liked. So, if I'm in the mood to try a new white wine, I'll tell the sommelier I don't want anything that resembles a Riesling.

Also, make sure to tell your sommelier whether you're feeling like a big spender or not. While most sommeliers don't try to push expensive wines, you may get steered toward something that isn't in your budget if you don't tell her what price range you're thinking.

Dining with a client or taking a friend out for her birthday and want to keep your budget on the DL? Point to a few of the wines you have in mind on the list. The sommelier will know you are discreetly communicating your budget and will make her recommendations accordingly.

DID YOU KNOW...If you are ordering for a large group: Assume two people per bottle of wine (this is roughly two glasses of wine each).

WHAT TO DO IF THERE IS NO SOMMELIER

If there is no sommelier or knowledgeable wine person at the restaurant, there are a few tricks to reading a wine menu and choosing a good wine on your own.

CONSIDER HOW THE WINE WILL PAIR WITH YOUR ENTRÉE: The number-one food and wine pairing rule is to make sure that neither one overpowers the other. If you are eating something light, choose a lighter-bodied wine; if you are eating something rich and heavy, choose a fuller-bodied wine. Sparkling wines and Rieslings are known for being great with spicy foods, while tannic reds are known for pairing well with dishes high in animal fat (such as steak). Anything with a lemon sauce pairs nicely with a high-acidity wine, because the acid cuts through the flavors and cleanses the palate.

ORDER A BOTTLE FROM ONE OF YOUR FAVORITE PRODUCERS: If I don't recognize any wines on a wine list, I typically look to see if I recognize any of the producers. For example, Ramey Wine Cellars (a Sonoma winery) makes one of my favorite Chardonnays. So, one time while dining out, I opted to try the Ramey claret red wine (a blend). Sure enough, that same "Ramey quality" of soft, round textures I'd come to love was also present in that amazing claret.

LOOK FOR A FAMILIAR WINE REGION: If you don't recognize any wines or producers on a list, look for a region you know you love. I love California wines, so if I have nothing else to go on, I'll look for wines from a region or appellation in California. Just keep in mind the smaller the appellation, the higher the quality of the wine, and as quality increases so does price. So you might want to bust out your appellation knowledge when you're on a date with someone who enjoys fine wines and doesn't mind paying for them.

GO AHEAD AND BE CHEAP: There is nothing wrong with the cheapest wine on the menu. No restaurant owner or sommelier will put a wine on the wine list that is of poor quality.

WINE-LIST BUZZWORDS THAT'LL HELP YOU

Here's your mini cheat sheet when it comes to the words you won't see anywhere except on a wine list:

VV: This indicates a vintage-dated wine, but you will need to ask your server for the vintage. Restaurants use this abbreviation so they don't have to constantly reprint their menus.

NV: This indicates a non-vintage wine, meaning the wine is a blend of wines from several harvest years (this is typical of Champagne). Whether a wine is vintage or a non-vintage isn't critical information to focus on when choosing a bottle—that is unless you memorize vintages like guys memorize sports trivia.

HOUSE WINES: Most restaurants will have one house white wine and one house red wine, and these are usually their least expensive wines. Ordering the "house white" or the "house red" is kind of like asking for the well vodka versus Grey Goose for your cranberry vodka.

DID YOU KNOW... If a restaurant allows you to bring your own bottle (BYOB), ask if they have a corkage fee. You'll especially want to know if they have a flat fee or a per-bottle fee. If possible, don't bring a wine that's on their menu—it's considered bad etiquette.

THE WINE-POURING RITUAL ▸ HOW TO LOOK LIKE YOU'VE BEEN A FRONT-ROW REGULAR ALL SEMESTER

Ah, the wine-pouring ritual. That silly, exaggerated process a server puts you through when he presents you with the wine you ordered.

I used to see this wine-pouring ritual as another opportunity to expose myself as a fraud, and it would remind me that I'm not from some fancy, pedigreed family. The worst part wasn't even the taste test at the end of the wine-pouring ritual; it was the part with the cork. When the server would daintily place the cork in front of me, I'd pause thinking, Uh-oh, am I supposed to do something with it? Sniff it? Examine it? Lick it? (Hint: You are not supposed to lick it.)

Although this ritual may seem a little ridiculous, knowing the purpose of each step and what you're expected to do will prevent you from looking clueless at the dinner table.

STEP 1 ▶ THE SERVER SHOWS YOU THE LABEL

WHY?

To confirm she brought you the correct bottle.

WHAT TO DO:

Make sure the label and the vintage match what you ordered.

One time while out to dinner with my mom, our bill was more than we anticipated. When we asked about the overcharge, we learned the server had accidentally brought us a more expensive vintage of the wine we ordered. Unfortunately, because we gave the server the nod that she brought us the correct one, we had to pay the extra cost.

STEP 2 ▶ THE SERVER OPENS THE BOTTLE OF WINE AND PLACES THE CORK IN FRONT OF YOU

WHY?

To show you the label on the cork matches the label on the bottle.

WHAT TO DO:

Take a glance at the cork if you'd like; otherwise just ignore it.

A long time ago, restaurateurs would put crappy wine into empty wine bottles with sought-after labels and seal it with a new cork. When these well-respected wineries caught on to what was happening, they labeled their corks. This way, customers would know if they were being ripped off.

Today, this never happens, but the tradition of showing the cork has lingered. It's kind of like how traditional wedding ceremonies still have the bit about the wife "obeying" her husband. Although the days of obedience are long gone (let's face it, we would need *much* larger diamonds for that), the tradition remains.

DID YOU KNOW...Some people think they need to smell the cork to check the wine's condition. Truth is, you'll get a much better idea of the wine's condition by smelling the wine, not the cork, so it's not necessary to sniff it.

STEP 3 ▸ THE SERVER POURS SOME WINE IN THE GLASS FOR YOU TO TASTE

WHY?

So you can judge if the wine is in good or bad condition.

WHAT TO DO:

You can choose to swirl or not swirl here, but definitely stick your nose in that glass and take a big whiff. It is the best way to know if the wine is in good condition or not. You can taste the wine if you'd like (most people do), and as long as the wine is in good condition, you can respond with a nod or "This is great."

The point of this step is to make sure nothing is wrong with the wine. This is not a "try before you buy" taste test. If the wine isn't your favorite—but it is in good condition—then better luck next time.

Step 3 is not a "try before you buy" taste test

However, don't be afraid to speak up if the wine smells or tastes funky. A bad bottle of wine will have a musty basement aroma (this is called being "corked"), or a vinegary aroma (this is called being "oxidized"). These aromas indicate the cork may have cracked, letting air into the wine, or the wine could have been damaged from improper storage.

If you taste the wine and are unsure about its condition, Lisa Hemmat suggests asking the restaurant sommelier to try it because they have a trained palate and will know if something is wrong with the wine.

Hemmat also says people often mistake sediment or tartaric acid as flaws and send the wine back. However, neither indicates a wine is in bad condition. Sediment is grape particles (tannins, seeds, and so on) that sit at the bottom of an unfiltered wine. Although most wines are filtered to remove the sediment, some smaller wineries choose to make their wines unfiltered for style.

Tartaric acid, on the other hand, is first noticeable on the cork in the form of crystals that look like glass or snowflakes. These tartaric acid crystals appear in wines that have not been cold stabilized. All you need to know about these little crystals is that they are harmless. As long as the wine smells and tastes fine, you are good to go.

STEP 4 ▶ FINALLY, THE SERVER POURS GLASSES OF WINE FOR EVERYONE AT YOUR TABLE (AND TYPICALLY THE WOMEN FIRST) BEFORE COMING BACK TO FILL YOUR GLASS

WHY?

This is considered proper wine-serving etiquette.

WHAT TO DO:

Before you question the server for giving you a chintzy pour, hang tight. The server will come back around and give you a full pour.

Next Up

➔ Get some wine-tasting party tips so you can start practicing your new skills with your friends. Now, who said learning wasn't fun?

➔ The final word on how long a wine will last after it's opened.

➔ Modern-day etiquette tips from Emily Post's great-great granddaughter, Anna Post.

ch 7

Practice makes Perfect

HOW TO HOST A KILLER WINE-TASTING PARTY

There is no better way to practice your swirling and wine-speak than by hosting a wine-tasting party with your girlfriends.

When I host a wine-tasting party, I try to reduce tasting anxiety by encouraging my friends to get as ridiculous as they can with their wine adjectives. Giving them permission to have fun with it allows everyone to actually describe what they taste instead of what they think they're *supposed* to taste.

Sometimes we make it a competition of who can come up with a better description than "Slim Jim," "pancakes," or "cat pee on a gooseberry bush." And the more wine we drink, the more awesome our buzzwords get. Check out some of our best buzzwords by looking up the hashtag **#MYBUZZWORDISBETTERTHANYOURS** on Instagram, and share yours, too.

Ready to get your buzzwords on? Here are the steps to follow to host a killer wine-tasting party.

STEP 1 ▸ GET YOUR CHECKLIST HANDY
Check out SavvyGirl.net for this pinnable checklist

Wine-Tasting Party Checklist

○ Choose a tasting theme (more on this later)

○ Keep the number of wines to six or fewer

○ Get the right glassware

○ Have a dump bucket for spitting out the yucks

○ Use an ice bucket if you are tasting white wines, rosés, or sparkling wines

○ Stock up on some palate cleansers, such as crackers or pretzels

○ Dust off the decanter for any young, tannic red wines

○ Place a pitcher of drinking water on the table to keep your friends from getting sloshed

○ Get Wine Away—the must-have carpet and upholstery spray cleaner for the inevitable red wine spills

STEP 2 ▸ GET THE RIGHT GLASSWARE
Not to go all wine snob on you, but wine tastes best when you're using the right glasses. Remember, most of what we taste is actually what we smell, so you'll want glasses you can swirl. If you try to swirl wine that's in a red plastic Solo cup or those hand-me-down mugs your mom gave you, the wine might land in your lap. Proper glassware—any clear glasses with stems—will optimize the whole see-swirl-sniff-sip experience.

DID YOU KNOW...If you're tasting sparkling wines at your party a typical wineglass is fine, but if you serve a sparkling wine (as a drink) you'll want to get some Champagne flutes—and not just because they look pretty. The narrow flute shape helps minimize bubble loss.

What about stemless wineglasses? Winos frown upon these because our hands warm up the wine in the glass. If you want my opinion, I love this type of wineglass because, well, it fits in my dishwasher.

STEP 3 ▸ GET THE ICE BUCKET, AND KNOW YOUR PROPER SERVING TEMPS

It's easy to forget an ice bucket when you're hosting a wine-tasting party, and you'll regret it as soon as your white wines get warm and icky-tasting (warm white wine can taste unbalanced). Get an inexpensive ice bucket from Target or a fancy one from Pottery Barn, and don't forget about buying ice if you don't have an icemaker.

Now, a couple rules of thumb for proper serving temperatures:

#1: SERVE WHITE WINES, SPARKLING WINES, AND ROSÉS CHILLED AND RED WINES AT ROOM TEMPERATURE.

I realize this is obvious, but I've got a friend who puts her Cabs in the fridge—and chilling red wines makes tannins taste bitter. One caveat: Lighter-bodied reds, like Pinot Noirs, are less tannic, so they can be slightly chilled. Stick those in the fridge ten minutes before serving.

#2: THE LIGHTER-BODIED A WINE IS, THE MORE IT CAN BE CHILLED.

The bottom line here is to not overchill your full-bodied whites. If you do, their flavors will seem muted. To keep your full-bodied whites (like your Chardonnays) full of flavor, pull them out of the fridge ten minutes prior to serving.

STEP 4 ▸ TO DECANT OR NOT TO DECANT?

Pouring red wine into a decanter with a large surface area allows more oxygen to mix with the wine, as opposed to just uncorking the bottle (not much air can get through that tiny neck). The mixing of the wine with oxygen triggers a chemical reaction that changes the wine's flavors. Essentially, it speeds up the aging process that improves a red

Make those harsh tannins purr

wine. As I'm sure you're about to guess, too much exposure to oxygen will cause a wine to oxidize and smell like vinegar. Thirty minutes to a few hours is fine, but don't leave your wine in a decanter overnight

WHAT WINES SHOULD YOU DECANT IF YOU'RE GOING TO DO IT?
Red wines, especially young tannic red wines (think Cabs), where the tannins haven't yet integrated into the wine. The contact with oxygen allows the tannins to soften, making the wine taste more "approachable" (wine-speak for "easier to drink").

A fun experiment for your wine-tasting parties would be to open two of the same wines, decant one, then try it side by side with the other and see if you and your friends can taste the difference.

STEP 5 ▸ PICK YOUR TASTING FLIGHT THEME

I always pick a theme for my tasting parties. I find it's much easier to compare and contrast wines if they are related to one another in some way.

- ▸ **VARIETAL THEME**: Such as Rieslings, Pinot Noirs, or Merlots
- ▸ **REGIONAL THEME**: Such as Cabs from Washington, whites from California, or reds from France
- ▸ **"NEW" WINES THEME**: Have everyone bring a varietal or country/region/appellation they haven't tried yet
- ▸ **WINE & CHEESE PAIRING THEME**: French wines and French cheeses, Spanish wines and Spanish cheeses, etc.
- ▸ **BLIND TASTING FLIGHT**: Compare wines with no known information about them. See who can guess the varietal correctly, or which wine is the most expensive (try covering the wine bottles with foil and labeling them with a Post-it note)

Or, try tasting wines side by side to learn specific buzzwords: Put an oaked Chardonnay next to an unoaked Chardonnay, or a sweet wine next to a dry wine, or a light-bodied wine next to a full-bodied wine. Check out the **BONUS CHAPTER** available at **SAVVYGIRL.NET** for some sample buzzword-themed flights.

TIPS ON WINE & CHEESE PAIRING

Norbert Wabnig, the owner of the Cheese Store of Beverly Hills, shares some of his best tips on wine and cheese pairing.

"First, you want to make sure the wine and the cheese don't overpower each other," says Wabnig. "For example, do not pair a stinky cheese with a delicate, light-bodied white wine."

"Second, the best wine and cheese pairings are when the wines and the cheeses are from the same region, because they have an amazing way of pairing together. This means pair French cheeses with French wines, Spanish cheeses with Spanish wines."

I told Wabnig this sounded obvious, but he explained that there's a story behind it: the cheese maker and the winemaker are both essentially farmers who lived next door to each other for many generations. As winemakers perfected their craft, so did cheese makers and they were both probably attending the same dinners and events. Naturally, the making of these specific wines and cheeses evolved so they would pair nicely with each other.

Touché, Wabnig.

savvy tip — Picking cheeses for a cheese plate can be surprisingly intimidating. Here is my personal trick: I pick out one soft cheese, one hard cheese, and one exotic cheese (meaning I can't pronounce it or have never heard of it). How do you know what cheeses are soft and what cheeses are hard? Touch 'em. Also, if you want to make the cheese plate look pretty, all you need are a few almonds, some red grapes, and maybe a sprig of rosemary.

STEP 6 ▸ FIGURE OUT THE TASTING ORDER

Basically, you want to taste whites before reds, light-bodied wines before full-bodied wines, and dry wines before sweet wines. Sweet wines will make dry wines taste bitter, and the richer flavors of full-bodied wines will mask the delicate flavors of a lighter wine.

STEP 7 ▸ HAVE YOUR SMART PHONE HANDY

Get your smart phones out and Instagram your "yums" and "yucks" with the hashtag **#YUMORYUCK** to see what other people love or hate. It'll help you know what to try or skip at your next wine-tasting adventure.

WHAT TO DO WITH WINE YOU DON'T FINISH

I wish I could give you an exact number of days until a wine turns, but I can't, because the pace depends on how much air is in the bottle.

Some sources say wine stays good for up to two days after opening it, while others say three days. I usually keep my wines up to three days, but some have lasted longer. The bottom line: Take a test sip. If the wine tastes fine, you're good to go. If it's turned, it'll smell and taste "off."

To slow the oxidation process and make your wine last longer, recork your wine and store it in the refrigerator. That advice goes for both white *and* red wines, by the way. Just make sure the reds get to room temp before you serve them.

As for unopened bottles, store them horizontally (if they have corks and if you don't plan to drink them within the next month). This keeps the cork moist so it doesn't dry out and crack. If the cork cracks, air will get in and oxidize the wine.

HOSTING ETIQUETTE TIPS

For some modern-day hosting etiquette ideas, I spoke with Bren Underwood, the author of my favorite etiquette blog, *Must Bring Buns*. Here are some of her hostessing tips:

USE INVITATIONS: "Invitations are a nice touch," Underwood says. She recommends services like Paperless Post for sending inexpensive and beautiful digital invitations.

SERVE PEOPLE SOMETHING BEFORE THE TASTING STARTS: Since you'll want to wait on the wine until everyone arrives before beginning the tasting, Underwood suggests serving people a glass of sparkling water with ice and a lime—something to sip on, but something that won't get them tipsy before the tasting. Try to avoid anything sweet, since it could make the wines you'll have later taste bitter. If you want to serve wine while everyone is waiting, a dry sparkling wine is a great choice.

DON'T FORGET ABOUT THE PEOPLE WHO AREN'T DRINKING: Provide nonalcoholic beverages for those who don't drink or aren't drinking that night. Lemonade, soda, or sparkling water with a lime are all great options. "The most important job of the hostess is to make sure everyone feels comfortable," says Underwood.

TRICKY SITUATIONS FOR THE HOSTESS AND HOW TO HANDLE THEM

Since I have also run into some "tricky" issues while hosting a wine-tasting party, I called Anna Post, a modern etiquette expert and coauthor of *Emily Post's Etiquette 18th Edition* (she's Emily Post's great-great granddaughter . . . etiquette is in her blood). She filled me in on the proper way to handle the trickiest hosting dilemmas:

Q: MODERN LADIES ARE HARD WORKERS AND OFTEN WORK LATE. SINCE A WINE-TASTING PARTY IS BEST WHEN EVERYONE STARTS THE TASTING TOGETHER, WHAT SHOULD I DO ABOUT GUESTS ARRIVING AT DIFFERENT TIMES?

Post says to specify what time your guests can start arriving (such as 7 p.m.) in your invitation as well as the tasting start time (i.e., "The wine-tasting portion will begin promptly at 8 p.m."). That way if someone is late, the whole group isn't waiting on that person.

Q: MY GUESTS ALWAYS OFFER TO BRING A WINE WHEN I HOST A WINE-TASTING PARTY, BUT WHAT IF I ALREADY BOUGHT THE WINES AND HAVE A SPECIFIC PLAN FOR WHICH WINES I'D LIKE TO SERVE? IF GUESTS STILL INSIST ON HELPING OUT, CAN I ASK PEOPLE TO CHIP IN A FEW BUCKS?

It's a definite no-no to ask people to give you cash, says Post. The best way to give people a chance to participate as well as reduce the financial burden on you when you've already purchased the wine is to ask your guests to bring some cheese or another snack (those palate cleansers, perhaps).

Q: HOW DO YOU INDICATE TO YOUR GUESTS THAT THE TASTING IS OVER AND IT'S TIME TO GO HOME?

While you obviously never want to ask someone to leave, Post says you can use subtle cues that'll let your guests know it's time to go home, such as turning off the music or starting to clear the food and glassware. People usually get the hint after that. Post also adds that putting an end time on your invitation can also set the expectation ahead of time for when the party will be over.

THE WINE-COUNTRY GETAWAY ▸ WHAT TO KNOW BEFORE YOU GO

No girls' trip gets me quite as excited as a getaway to wine country. Each time I see the rolling hills of beautiful vineyards, feel the warm

breezes of the countryside, and taste my first sips of delicious vino, I start to daydream about whether any of the winemakers' sons might be single....

Whether your next wine-tasting trip is focused on getting tipsy with your girlfriends, getting savvy about wine, or finding a future winemaking hubby (or all of the above), there are a few things to know before you go.

THE WINE-TASTING GETAWAY CHECKLIST

- ○ **VISIT NO MORE THAN THREE WINERIES EACH DAY.** Trust me on this one. After you've tasted about five wines per winery, you'll be totally over it by the fourth winery.
- ○ **SEE A VARIETY OF WINERIES.** Some wineries have cool tours, others have scenic views, and some have art galleries.
- ○ **ARRANGE FOR TRANSPORTATION.** You already know that it's not cool to drink and drive, so join a guided tour or arrange for a driver so you can sit back and enjoy. Cheap out on the hotel instead; you won't be spending much time there anyway.

- ○ **KNOW THE DISTANCE BETWEEN THE WINERIES YOU VISIT.** Find ones that are close to each other, otherwise you may find yourself rushing through tastings so you're not late for the next one.
- ○ **BE AWARE OF HIDDEN COSTS.** Most tastings and winery tours cost money and those fees can range considerably. Check out the winery's website ahead of time so you are aware of these costs.
- ○ **MAKE APPOINTMENTS.** Many wineries are open only on certain days of the week, and several high-profile wineries require appointments ahead of time. You don't want to drive forty-five minutes to a winery just to realize they're closed or all of their tastings are booked for the day.
- ○ **MAKE LUNCH PLANS.** You'll need some grub to counteract all that alcohol. Either ask your driver to pick up some sandwiches or make plans to stop at a local restaurant.
- ○ **CHECK OUT BOUTIQUE WINERIES.** Larger wineries can sometimes seem a little touristy. Boutique wineries are less crowded, and you'll receive more personalized attention.
- ○ **CHECK OUT OTHER FUN THINGS TO DO.** Fine dining, hot air balloon rides, spa treatments, bike riding—wine country has it all.

When you go wine tasting, remember that there is no pressure to purchase the wine or join their wine club. Only buy the wine if you really want it.

Another great piece of advice for wine getaways is to consider going on an organized tour. After all, "great wine doesn't always mean a great visit," says Peter Smith, contributor to the *Sommelier Journal* and founder of Avalon Wine Tours. Specialist wine tour operators know the wineries to avoid and the hidden gems that will make your visit amazing.

Going with a wine guide or small group can be a great option, especially if you are traveling overseas. However, if you plan your own trip, Smith recommends making appointments ahead of time instead of stopping by. "Visitors are always treated better when the winery knows in advance that they are coming," he says.

MY PERFECT DAY IN NAPA ▶ A SAMPLE ITINERARY

To make the getaway planning less work and more fun, here is my
favorite itinerary for a day in Napa:

11 A.M. *Begin at Del Dotto*

Del Dotto has the best tour, in my
opinion. The wine cave tour takes
you through hand-carved caves built
in the 1880s, where Del Dotto stores
their wines for aging in American and
French oak barrels. As you tour the
candlelit caves, your tour guide will
draw some wine out of the barrels for you to
taste. Although the cave tour is a little pricey, it's worth it. The caves
are magical and Del Dotto's wine is out of this world.

1 P.M. *Arrive at
V. Sattui for
lunch*

V. Sattui is the perfect lunch stop. You can bring your own picnic
or purchase food and eat it on their gorgeous grounds. They also
have a tasting room where you can buy wine to have with lunch.
The only downfall is that this place gets jam-packed with tourists
in the summer.

3 P.M. Arrive at Castello di Amorosa

Castello di Amorosa is a Tuscan-style castle in the middle of Napa. It took fourteen years to build because the owners wanted it to be as authentic as possible. You can tour the castle's interior and then head underground to their romantic tasting room, filled with seductive Italian wines. Oh, and the sexy Italian guys behind the tasting table aren't bad either.

6 TIPS ON HOW TO SOUND SAVVY WHILE WINE TASTING

1. **ASK QUESTIONS.** I promise, you don't need to recite wine facts to sound savvy about wine. The people behind the tasting bar love it when people ask questions instead of downing the wine in one sip and reaching for the next pour. Asking questions about the wine shows you're interested in wine and savvy enough to know there is more to wine than alcohol.

2. **ASK IF THE CHARDONNAY WENT THROUGH MALOLACTIC FERMENTATION.** Malo (or ML, as it's also referred to) is a "nerd" wine term. So if you ask if there was any malo, there's a good chance you'll see the tasting bar guy's face light up. It might even get you an extra pour.

3. **ASK ABOUT THE USE OF OAK BARRELS.** What type of oak they used and why.

4. **ASK ABOUT BLENDS.** Blends tend to make fantastic wines because the winemaker has more freedom and control over the resulting flavor profile. In other words, a blend is a winemaker's work of art.

Ask the winemaker why he wanted to make that blend and why he chose those particular grapes.

5. ASK ABOUT THE TERROIR. Trust me here: The same way all parents think their kid is the cutest, winemakers think their terroir is the best. They would *love* the opportunity to tell you about it, and maybe even show you a photo. Also, ask about how the weather affected the vintage you are drinking. This will show the winemaker you "appreciate" wine and she might even pour you a taste of another vintage so you can try them side by side.

6. FINALLY, DON'T WORRY ABOUT TRYING TO FIND THAT "HINT OF GRASS." Try to use the buzzwords you've learned in this book, but don't worry about looking for all the aromas listed in the tasting notes. After all, those tasting notes are somebody else's experience of what the wine tastes like. Just keep your buzzwords simple and try to describe why it is yum or yuck to you.

Acknowledgments

This book would not have been possible without the dedication, hard work, creativity, and patience of the following people:

Content Editor: **MEGHAN RABBITT**

Copyeditor: **RACHELLE MANDIK**

Cover and Interior Designer: **TARA LONG**

A SPECIAL THANKS . . .

TO MEGHAN: I think I won the content-editor Lotto. You have incredible judgment, and your feedback was invaluable in the creation of this book. Thanks for always being honest with me and never letting me get away with a lazy paragraph.

TO TARA: Wow! I got incredibly lucky in finding you! You are so talented at design. The cover and interior of this book turned out better than I ever imagined. Thanks for all your hard work.

TO THE EXPERTS QUOTED IN THIS BOOK: Thanks for being open to an interview. Your input made this book better, and I am incredibly thankful.

TO LOU: You are the love of my life, the most handsome man in the world, and my sunshine on a rainy day. You inspire me more than you'll ever know, but what is even more important is you aren't afraid to challenge me. I feel so lucky to have found a true partner and best friend to share my life with.

TO MY FAMILY: You made this book a possibility because of your love and support. Thanks for supporting my crazy ideas, and for your continued faith in me.

TO MY GIRLFRIENDS: I couldn't ask for a smarter, more beautiful and fun group of friends.

TO BETSY: In Stephen King's book *On Writing*, he talks about writing with your "Ideal Reader" in mind. Not only were you the best beta reader ever, but you were also my "Ideal Reader."

A quote that inspired me throughout this process:

It doesn't get easier, we just get better
—John Hering, CEO of Lookout

Cheers to us all working toward getting better!

Bibliography

The following books were used in my research for this book.

Kamp, David, and David Lynch. *The Wine Snob's Dictionary.* New York: Broadway Books, 2008.

MacNeil, Karen. *The Wine Bible.* New York: Workman Publishing, Inc., 2001.

McCarthy, Ed, and Mary Ewing-Mulligan. *Wine for Dummies.* Hoboken, NJ: John Wiley & Sons, Inc., 2012.

Nowak, Barbara, and Beverly Wichman. *The Everything Wine Book.* Avon, MA: Adams Media, 2005.

Robinson, Jancis. *How to Taste.* New York: Simon & Schuster, 2008.

Schuster, Michael. *Essential Winetasting.* London: Mitchell Beazley, 2009.

Simonetti-Bryan, Jennifer. *The One Minute Wine Master.* New York: Sterling Epicure, 2012.

Zraly, Kevin. *Complete Wine Course.* New York: Sterling Epicure, 2011.

A note from the author

Thanks for reading! And don't forget to share your yums, or yucks, with me on Instagram!

XO
Brittany

TWITTER & INSTAGRAM:
@BrittanyDeal425
@SAVVYGIRLguides
#yumoryuck
#SavvyGirl
#SavvyGirlWine

WANT MORE SAVVY GIRL?
Savvy Girl is a guidebook series written for women about topics we care about.

If you enjoyed this book, visit savvygirl.net and sign up to be notified when the next Savvy Girl guidebook is published.

INTERESTED IN COLLABORATING WITH SAVVY GIRL?
Are you an expert on a topic? Contact me via Savvygirl.net about collaborating on a Savvy Girl guide book or future Savvygirl.tv videos.

Photo Credits

COVER PHOTOS

cork ©Lilybranch, *stain* ©Picsfive

INTERIOR PHOTOS

p. 3 ©Peeradach Rattanakoses ; p. 5 ©marslasarphotos;
p. 7 ©Morphart Creation; p. 9 ©Ferenc Cegledi, ©Jorg Hackemann,
© visuall2; p. 12 ©Sydneymills; p. 17 ©Zhukov Oleg;
p. 19 ©Tamara Kulikova; p. 20 ©gresei; p. 24 *top left to bottom right*
©ifong, ©unverdorben jr, ©Dino Osmic, ©Volosina, ©Volosina,
©Teresa Azevedo, ©Nattika; p. 26 ©Picsfive; p. 32 ©kosit limsiri;
p. 37 ©Theo Fitzhugh; p. 45 ©Natalia Davydenko;
p. 50 ©Eldad Carin; p. 59 ©Denis Komarov; p. 60 ©Denis Komarov;
p. 61 ©Evgeny Karandaev; p. 72 ©Gyuszko-Photo; p. 77 ©Silberkorn;
p. 79 ©kiboka; p. 85 ©Dennis Albert Richardson

20738327R00055

Made in the USA
San Bernardino, CA
21 April 2015